MICHELLI

FOUNDER O

Enjoy the read!
Much love all the
way from Australia.
Michelle

PARENTING TEENAGE GIRLS

IN THE AGE OF A NEW NORMAL

ARK house

Ark House Press
PO Box 1722, Port Orchard, WA 98366 USA
PO Box 1321, Mona Vale NSW 1660 Australia
PO Box 318 334, West Harbour, Auckland 0661 New Zealand
arkhousepress.com

Cataloguing in Publication Data:
Title: Parenting Teenage Girls in the Age of a New Normal
ISBN: 9780648084525 (pbk.)
Subjects: Parenting
Other Authors/Contributors: Mitchell, Michelle

Design and Layout by initiateagency.com

Michelle's insight and knowledge about teenagers and their experiences are invaluable for parents. Her ideas are practical and sensible while being loving and understanding – the perfect mix for parenting today's teenage girls. I highly recommend Michelle's expertise to parents who are embarking on these challenging years.

Carmel Nash

Executive Director - Queensland Parents & Friends Federation, Catholic Education

Michelle has a way of telling parents how it is, why it is and what to do about it! This practical empowerment guide is essential reading for every parent with teens and pre-teens, especially girls. The passion poured into this book should be enough to get every parent inspired to not just survive, but thrive through the Twilight Zone years!

Dr Robi Sonderegger

Humanitarian Activist and Clinical Psychologist

In her new book Michelle delivers a timely reminder that we are entering an unprecedented phase of adolescent turmoil. Never before have young people had such power in their hands while often lacking the cognitive maturity to make appropriate decisions. Parents can no longer afford to sit on the technological sidelines with their child's moral and intellectual integrity is at stake. Drawing on many years of personal experience Michelle offers parents many clear, relevant and proven insights to guide their teenagers through these uncharted waters. The time to up-skill has arrived and this book will provide timely reassurance for anxious parents everywhere.

Dale Dearman

Head of Student Support, Grace Lutheran College

I stand in awe of Michelle's incredible energy, passion and relentless desire to empower our girls. Her latest book contains real life stories, relevant advice and researched facts that will assist parents in the roller coast ride of parenting a teenager. As a mother of girls and a women's health care professional for over twenty years, Michelle's book is one you do not want to miss.

Karen Spatuzzo

Registered Nurse / Mother of Teenage Girls

I have read a lot of parenting books that made me feel that we were maybe doing things wrong, maybe not doing enough or even possibly doing too much. Michelle's book was different. I found myself nodding the whole time. At times, I read with a lump in my throat thinking, "We aren't the only ones and we are doing lots of things right!" I also picked up a lot of insightful tips and strategies I could put to use straight away and some I have stored away for when I might need them (hopefully I never need them!!!)

Stephanie Foster

Parent of three

Foreword

As the director of Teen Challenge, I understand first-hand the importance of the work that Michelle does. At Teen Challenge we specialise in helping young people who are struggling with addictions. Our youth workers stand at the bottom of the cliff to catch these young people who have fallen into a devastating lifestyle of drug and alcohol addiction, self-harm and eating disorders.

Parenting Teenage Girls in the Age of a New Normal helps parents build a fence at the top of the cliff and prevent teenagers from a lifestyle of poor choices. Early intervention is critical in helping young people avoid addictions and to grow strong lives. I highly commend Michelle for all she is doing on the frontline of youth work in these formative years.

The teen years can be a daunting and confusing time for parents. I'm sure there are times that each one of us wished we'd had a textbook that could guide us during the difficult moments of parenting our children. *Parenting Teenage Girls in the Age of a New Normal* is one of those 'go to' books. It is a powerful resource and valuable tool to help parents understand the challenging issues that their teenagers are facing today.

Parenting Teenage Girls in the Age of a New Normal certainly doesn't avoid the tough issues and you will find real and practical information and advice on topics like disrespect, social media, sexuality, moods and drugs and alcohol within this book's pages. Each chapter opens with eye opening statistics, which shoot straight to the heart of the issue.

Michelle's thoughts on each topic are at times humorous and other times saddening. They are however, always grounded in her day-to-day experiences and work with young people and followed by practical, useable strategies. Michelle also details anecdotes from parents who are interacting with her work on a daily basis. It is this balance of time-tested advice as it interacts with real families, which makes this book so relatable.

Technology, and social media in particular, is such a concern for parents today and Michelle has so clearly and practically discussed this topic as to allow every parent insight and strategies to guide their teenagers or pre-teenagers. I believe it is critical that parents are well informed in this area so we can set clear boundaries and intelligently discuss these issues with our teenagers.

Thank you Michelle for giving us such insight into some very complex issues and for helping us to build resilience into our children. Your work on the frontline of youth issues is to be highly commended.

I highly recommend this book to all parents.

Joanne Hobbs
Executive Director of Teen Challenge QLD

Table of Contents

Thank You

I want to take this opportunity to thank all the families who have shared their lives with me over the past fifteen years, and those who have taken the time to contribute to this book in the last few months. Thank you to the mums who 'wrote in' and 'facebooked in' to add some real and practical elements to each strategy. You never know whose life you may touch or the difference you may make by simply sharing yourself with someone else.

Thank you also to my staff for the life changing work you are doing everyday with young people and their families. I am constantly learning and growing as I watch you in action. I appreciate you, your insights and your help with the research and imagery for this book. May we continue to support families together for many years to come.

INTRODUCTION

I Have Met Your Daughter

There are times when I choose to make house calls. One night I visited the home of Lucy, a 14 year-old girl who was attending one of Youth Excel's school programs. I was finding it difficult to put my finger on what was going on in this girl's life, so I decided to pop over to talk to her mother and father and get their perspective. As I approached the front door swung open to greet me.

"Oh Michelle, my daughter has told me so much about you. Please, please come in." Mum hugged me and shook my hand simultaneously as she hurried me through the front door. Lucy was all smiles to see me outside of school hours so she showed me her bedroom.

Before long, Lucy's mum asked Lucy to disappear so she and her husband could talk to me in private. I remember staying late into the night listening to stories that Lucy's parents felt were unique to their family... stories of teenage defiance, selfishness, manipulation, irrational thinking, rudeness and tantrums.

Mum spoke to me about Lucy's blatant disrespect. 'No' and 'whatever' seemed to be words that Lucy liked to use regularly which irritated the living heck out of her mother. Lucy couldn't seem to say anything nice to anyone, especially her younger brother who was being crushed by her vicious tongue.

Both her parents shared concerns about social media and the constant stream of try-hard 'sexy' photos, which her friends posted. Dad was concerned about the amount of time she was spending online and told me he had even caught her taking her mobile phone to the bathroom, which he thought was beyond ridiculous!

I listened to stories about Lucy's attempts to meet boyfriends at 'late night' when she was supposed to be shopping with her girlfriends. I mean, what was she thinking? She wasn't brought up like this. Then there were constant fights about skirts that were 'too short' and tops that were 'too low', and invites to parties, which she insisted that 'everyone else was going to'.

I could feel Lucy's parents' frustration rise when they began to talk about Lucy's lack of regard for *their* money. Her bedroom was already overflowing with clothes, shoes, bags and jewellery, most of which she rarely wore let alone looked after. Enough never seemed to be enough and dad was tired of feeling like an ATM.

It was obvious that mum was handling the brunt of the arguments while dad was at work. She was feeling both intimidated and inadequate. Lucy, however, seemed to remain blissfully unaware of her mum's feelings and thought it was her parents' personal stress levels that were causing the tension.

Lucy's parents' stories led them to a big finale where they leaned in close, lowered their voices and asked me in a very, very serious tone, "Do you think there is something wrong with her? I mean, is this normal?"

"Normal," I laughed (to myself of course!). "This is so *VERY* normal!"

You would be amazed how many parents ask me if I think that their daughter's behaviour is *normal*. If I were to be honest it's the question that I am asked the most often. I sometimes wonder if parents secretly hope that there is a medical condition to blame for the absolute nonsense that comes from their teenagers' mouths. That way they could at least give them a pill and it would be all over.

Where it is understandable (and very responsible) to be concerned about extreme behaviour, I want you to know that the vast majority of kids are living with the same condition as their peers – 21st century puberty. Unfortunately, there is no quick or easy cure. The only way through it is through it. As Nigel Latta brilliantly puts it, "The cure for 13 is 14 and the cure for 14 is 15."

If your daughter struggles with a sense of entitlement, a smart mouth, a premature discovery of her sexuality, a gravitational pull towards selfies and social media, a lack of empathy or difficulty regulating her emotions, be assured that you are not alone. We all think that everyone else's kids are somehow different than ours, but don't be fooled. Behind closed doors we are all concerned with the same issues. *I can't emphasise that enough.*

The one thing I find really amazing is how similar all the girls I work with actually are. They may look different, be developing at different rates, live in different socio-economic areas and go to different schools, but they are all very much alike because they are a part of a new and quickly evolving culture which is driven by technology.

For all those facts and figures people out there, national

statistics tell us that our girls are facing pressures and challenges that are unprecedented. We aren't just talking about perceived challenges hyped up by the media. Our girls really are struggling with specific issues that other generations have not faced in the same way.

- 36% of kids see pornography by the time they are 12 years old[1].
- 38% will send a nude before age 16, and 50% will send a nude before they are 18[2]
- 10% of young people will self-harm[3]
- 10% will drink alcohol weekly[4]
- 46% will be bullied[5]
- 14.4% of 12-17 year olds experience a mental illness[6]

These statistics resonate differently with different parents. Sometimes parents shed a tear when they hear them because they represent their daughter who is struggling. Other times parents nod in agreement because they represent their daughters' friends. Parents of pre-teens show genuine concern because they realise the upcoming years will present challenges they didn't anticipate. We all know that these statistics are not just numbers on a page. They represent young lives that all have a face, story and future.

A Unique Time in History

I recently visited my ninety-two year-old granny in the aged care facility where she now lives. I had arrived on a very special day. It was the annual piano accordion concert day, led by a short, grey haired woman who reintroduced me to words like jolly and gay. The atmosphere was electric. I was surrounded by involuntary dribble but I could tell I was about to have a great time.

Over the next hour I watched one hundred old people sing the greatest hits of 1920 with elderly vigour. It was their opportunity to relive their childhood memories. I soon realised that 'Pack up your troubles in an old kit bag' and 'Tie me kangaroo down' represented their life's experiences. These oldies were singing (and smiling) like they were 16 again.

As I sat there I was imagining what an old people's home would look like for this current generation of teenagers. If I could magically fast forward the clock sixty years what would I see? For one thing there would be a lot of wrinkled tattoos. That means an entire room full of shrunken ink. If you can get past that visual, ask yourself what would they be singing? What would be the anthem of their teenage years? It certainly won't be 'Pack up your troubles in an old kit bag'.

The 'good old days' had its own set of challenges, none which would have felt any less significant than the ones we are facing today. Their challenges included times of war, poverty, death and sickness. My great grandparents struggled with loss and grief on a level that I can't even imagine. I am also sure that the swinging 60s and the freelove 70s with an explosion of thrusting pelvises, drugs and feminism caused parents just as many sleepless nights as nowadays.

Yet equally, our girls have been born in a unique time in history and have a unique culture which defines them. They have been given experiences and opportunities that former generations could have only dreamt about, yet I believe it is safe to say they are also facing challenges which have not confronted any other generation in the same way.

It is amazing to consider how much our world has changed

over the last few generations. The normal teenager of yester year and today's teenager are two totally different species. Not only do they look different, they have different influences, experiences and ideas. While moodiness, tantrums and bucking the system are a normal part of growing up there are some new issues marking a change in teenage culture.

So, what is unique about this generation of girls?

They are educated. They live in a world where they have unlimited opportunity to learn.

They make up their own minds about social and moral issues. They can instantly access whatever information they need or want to help them make these decisions.

They have a complete and utter dependence on their phones, which keeps them constantly entertained and connects them to their friends 24/7, yet they are insecure and lonely.

They have been exposed to sexual content at a strikingly young age and that impacts their self-concept, body image and the way they want to dress.

They are hitting puberty earlier and earlier.[51] On average, girls have their first period when they are around 12.5 years old, but their body is changing and their breasts may start developing up to two years before this[7].

They are a consumer generation. They expect a high standard of living and easily compare themselves to reality television stars and other celebrities.

They live a fast pace life and have very little down time to process it all. They typically struggle with the management of their emotions, especially disappointments and anxiety. They have trouble accepting the word 'no'.

They have a social conscience that comes with access to international media and environmental studies.

They have been called a 'latch key' generation. Their parents (that's us) are super busy and often absent or disengaged when they are needed the most. Gulp!

It really is a new normal.

New Strategies for a New Normal

I have learnt a lot as I have written this book. One thing I have discovered is that *normal is not necessarily okay.* Parents aren't okay with the levels of depression and anxiety young people are experiencing. They are not okay with their daughters being exposed to pornographic images before they have even discovered what sex is. They don't turn on the news each night and feel okay about the aggression and disrespect that they see. Normal is not necessarily okay for your kids or mine.

However, I have noticed that once parents are convinced that something is socially accepted they often feel defeated. They don't fight very hard against something that 'everyone is doing' because they simply can't see themselves winning, even if they are deeply unhappy with it. Instead they throw their hands up in surrender. When I hear parents say, "I don't like it but I can't stop it" what they really mean is, "If all her friends are doing it, what chance do I have of saying no?"

The more time I spend with parents the more I realise how much they lack the confidence to tackle the big issues facing their pre-teens or teens. Perhaps this is because the strategies they saw their parents use don't transfer to some of the new issues facing this generation. Perhaps it is because their current parenting strategies are ineffective. I know that parents often feel clouded by tiredness or disabled by fear so they stop making decisions when they know they need to.

I have written this book in the hope that parents will know what to do when they usually wouldn't know what to do. I'd like to ensure that you don't just throw your hands up in forced surrender without any other options but defeat. I honestly believe that armed with more information parents can more confidently play a stronger role in their daughters' lives. I've seen a little knowledge go a long way.

While reading this book I hope you feel like you are sitting in my office, talking to me about your daughter. Just pull up a chair and pretend we are having a chat. You will notice that my advice is simple, practical and honest. My job is to help bring you back to basics when family life becomes complex.

Disrespect, social media, sexuality, moods and drugs and alcohol are the issues I am seeing families struggle with the most and therefore have become the chapters of this book. Once you get inside each chapter you will notice it will be divided into the following sections to enable you easy access to the content when you need it.

i. Snap Shot of Reality
Latest statistics affecting our teenagers.

ii. Basic Overview

My own thoughts about each issue based on my work with teenagers and their families.

iii. Parenting Strategies

Some very down to earth, practical parenting strategies. This section also has contributions from parents who have 'written in' to give their opinion about each strategy and whether it has worked in their household.

I want you to pick up this book with confidence knowing I have met your daughter. You will find her in these pages. I can also guarantee that as you read the many stories and letters from mothers in the coming chapters you will find yourself nodding in agreement time and time again. This book is all about you and your family. That is what makes it work.

Enjoy the read!

CHAPTER ONE

Disrespect

A Snap Shot of Reality

963 million people go to bed hungry every night[8] and 150 million children under 14 years old are engaged in child labour worldwide[9]. In comparison to the third world, our daughters live a life of privilege.

The number of teenagers refusing to pitch in has almost tripled from 5.6 per cent to 15.8 per cent. In 2006 the average time girls spent doing household tasks was 28 minutes a day. In 1992 it was 40 minutes a day. In 2006 nearly 16% of teenage girls did no housework at all. In 1992 the figure was only 5.6%[10].

87% of teenagers aged between 12 and 19 use curse words or foul language in their everyday conversations[11].

59% of teenagers report that they avoid, lie or only partially tell their parents the truth about hanging out with people that their parents think are problematic, hanging out with friends when adults are not around, and where they go with their friends[12].

Teenagers' belief in their parents' legitimacy and feelings of obligation to obey their parents decreases with age, with the biggest decline being in their early adolescence.

Teenagers who feel more supported and are well monitored by their parents are more likely to endorse parental legitimacy and obligation to obey their parents[13].

Teenagers aged 15-19 are more likely to be processed by police for the commission of a crime than members of any other population[14]. The offending rate of teenagers aged 15-19 is more than two and a half times the rate for other offenders[15]. For girls, the most likely age of conviction is 18 years old[16].

The Real Issue of Disrespect

I must confess to 'accidentally' overhearing a mother and daughter conversation at the movie theatre yesterday. It was taking place in the row behind me a few minutes before the movie started. The lights were dim so I didn't get a good look at the happy couple but they sounded like your standard mother-daughter type. I found myself so desperate to hear their whispers that I started chewing my popcorn very, very quietly and hoping the trailers wouldn't start on time.

The exchange went down something like this....

The teenage girl was concerned about whether her boyfriend would turn up or not. She had texted him earlier inviting him to join them and although she hadn't heard back from him she was hopeful of his arrival. The mother was annoyed that she had invited her boyfriend to an outing that was meant to be about them spending time together. In fact she didn't sound too keen on the boyfriend being around at all.

The expected backchat started.
Mum: You didn't ask me if you could invite Ryan.
Teenager: I shouldn't have to.
Mum: Don't speak to me like that!
Teenager: Speak to you like what?
Mum: You are speaking to me rudely.
Teenager: That's not rude!
Mum: We are trying to have a nice time. You are wrecking it.
Teenager: You are the one making a scene! Ryan can come if

he wants to. It's a public place. You can't stop him.
Mum: Be quiet!!!
Teenager: Or what? What are you going to do about it?

I could hear mum's internal dialogue over the noise of the trailers, "You rude little piece of work. Did you ever stop to consider that I am paying for *your* movie ticket?" My eyes kept glancing over at the 'exit' sign. I was silently hoping the boyfriend would walk through the entrance and join them. What a great story that would make. No such luck. The movie started, everyone was distracted and life returned to normal.

The number one thing that parents (and grandparents) talk to me about is their daughters' lack of respect for authority, money and things. When I hear parents say, "I would have never acted like that when I was fourteen," I totally believe them. They haven't simply forgotten what they got up to and they haven't developed Alzheimer's early. They literally mean, "There is no way in hell I would have ever spoken to my parents like that or I would have gotten a hiding."

One mother recently told me, "At 13 I had chores and I had to do them. I never questioned it. I was expected to help around the house. My daughter thinks it is abnormal for me to ask her to do jobs. She yells and screams if I ask her to clean her room or pick up her clothes like I am asking her to do something unreasonable. She thinks I am intruding on her internet or social time that is her divine right as a teenager!"

Another mother wrote to me saying, "When I was 15 I was working a part time job, baby sitting four young children. I would NEVER leave my 15-year-old alone with four children. She simply isn't responsible enough. She is so nasty to her younger sisters I can hardly believe it some days. I always helped around the house and I took care of my younger brothers and sisters. I felt responsible for them. My daughter can't even get herself out of bed on Saturday morning and I dare not ask her to help around the house... it's just not worth my effort!"

The thing that blows my mind is this: while parents are tearing their hair out girls actually don't think that they are being disrespectful. They just don't seem to hear themselves. They think it is normal to speak to their parents with a bit of attitude. I believe they call it 'banter' or 'speaking like they are spoken to'. They don't think it's a big deal at all. Think about it, how many times have you corrected your teenager for being disrespectful this week? Out of those times, how many times have they admitted that they were being disrespectful?

I am seeing more and more parents struggle to maintain authority in their homes, succumbing to a barrage of disrespect they just don't seem to be able to get on top of. Parents are genuinely concerned about their daughters' smart mouths and attitudes, stubborn defiance and non-compliant attitude, which would test the patience of any saint, let alone a tired mother after a hard day's work.

Unfortunately I am hearing more and more parents say, "When I finally say 'no' to my daughter she doesn't seem to hear this word. The backchat is constant and nothing I do seems to be working. I feel like I am missing the mark as the parent. I don't feel like I have any authority that my parents had when I was young."

I am also seeing more schools struggling to manage teenagers' disrespectful behaviour, which is obviously not isolated to females. This year I have personally witnessed more swearing, cursing, spitting and throwing things than ever before. Most times it's over the smallest of things, like whether they were talking in class or not, which makes you wonder whether disrespect has become a sport. One might ask what has happened to good old-fashioned respect that has held our families and communities together for centuries? And more importantly what can we do about bringing it back?

Who Are You in Your Daughter's Life?

Before we get up in arms about this generation's attitude, I think it is really important to stop and think about the culture that our daughters have been born into. When we were young we saw our parents as the final authority in our lives. There was little we could discover without them. We didn't have the Internet to teach us how the world worked. They and our school teachers were our source of knowledge. We relied on them. We revered and respected them because we believed they were all knowing and right.

Today, however, our children question all authority. Why? A teenager once said to me, "I don't need my parents to tell me what to believe, I have the internet. I can research whatever I want to and make an informed decision." This tells me a lot about this generation. Amongst all the information bombarding our daughters, parent's voices have become one voice amongst a multitude of voices. Research tells us that parents are still the most influential voice - but they are still only one voice. It is no wonder that parents feel like they are competing with the media, social media and even the school system in order to be heard. They rarely feel respected for their opinion or position.

I have noticed that children have strikingly strong opinions, which often differ from their parents at very young ages. I find myself listening to 12-year-olds arguing with their parents about things that I would have thought pointless to disagree with my parents about. It was assumed that I would do as my parents did until I was an adult. I hear 12-year-olds argue about whether they will attend church with their family, whether they agree with sex before marriage or whether they even want to go to school.

The policeman badge our parents used to wave around doesn't cut it for this generation of kids. They just pull out their research and argue us down to the ground. The 'because I said so' line that our parents used isn't acceptable or enough anymore. Our children debate with researched and substantiated arguments that would make any parent second-guess themselves. This is a hard position for parents.

That being said, we can't lose our confidence and stop guiding our daughters. Encouraging them to think critically while expecting them to respect and follow our moral compass until they develop enough life experiences to make their own choices is an interesting balance. But parents, I am actually begging you to have the courage to remain parents, even though I know you have a lot of competition.

When a teenager is caught sexting or is experiencing bullying I find that they look for a predictable, loving parent with a clear and confident voice. I have been with a lot of girls whose parents had found out they have done something 'inappropriate'. They all say the same thing to me: "I knew mum would react like that." The reaction, although most often involving discipline of some sort was almost comforting to them. It was a relief that they experienced exactly what they thought they would experience from them - protection, values and love.

I often feel that parents of this generation fear saying 'no' to their kids. Although I agree that it is ideal to engage in as little warfare as possible, if teenagers challenge your authority it is important that you meet those challenges and pass with flying colours. Although picking your battles is important, so is winning the little battles. If you don't win the little battles how will you ever win the big battles that matter?

Parents, please make tough decisions when you need to. Have the courage to say 'no'. These decisions aren't always popular decisions and I know that they aren't always easy. However, they firmly establish that you love your daughters in a way that no one else does or ever will! No one can replace you in their lives and without you, they may lose their way.

Not an Adult, Not a Child

The reality is that our children are not going to be children forever. We have a window of opportunity in which their brain is being wired for their adult life[17]. But as they move past the middle school years and into their senior years parenting dramatically changes. Teenagers are on the verge of becoming adults, leaving school, driving a car and earning their own money. They think they know everything and are ready for the real world. Parents may not be so sure.

These years are nerve racking for parents. Young people have so many very big decisions ahead of them. The outcome of those decisions will in some cases shape their futures. This is a weight that usually lies far heavier on parents than on teenagers.

Mothers, can I talk directly to you for a minute? We have to show confidence in our girls during this stage. Our confidence in them is critical to their success. You have taught them well, so let go in safe environments and trust that they will fly, even when if they are flying like a pigeon! Lacking confidence in them will only leave us hanging on to them and them hanging onto us. We can't try to control them out of fear that they will fail.

It is important (for your sanity and their sense of independence) to become less involved in the trivial, day-to-day management as they get older. Pulling back can be really hard for mums who have always packed their child a cut lunch and made sure they have packed their sunscreen, but we have to try (yes, I am a mum too). Talk less. Meddle less. Fuss less. Worry less. Supervise less. It takes a deliberate choice to ignore things that aren't important.

Real life lessons become their greatest teacher. If parents choose to let the real world take over, it is amazing to see the maturing that can happen. For this reason parents have to make sure they don't interfere with real world consequences. Don't pay their bills or speak on their behalf. Let them feel the weight of their decisions and learn to relate to the world for themselves. It may look a little messy for a while, but in the end it will pay off.

How much freedom is reasonable? Do I let them go to parties with alcohol? What time should they be home? Should they be allowed to drive with P plater drivers? Take some comfort in knowing that there are no right or wrong answers to any of these questions. To a certain degree I really do think it depends on the child themselves, their maturity and their stage of development at the time. Boundaries are going to need to be adjusted and continually re-negotiated as your teenager matures.

For parents, it will feel like change is happening at lightning speed. For teenagers, it will feel like change is happening at snail's pace. This is the push and pull of growing up. Boundaries are so individual to each family and are impacted by maturity, family structure, culture, peer influences and resilience. There is no doubt they are hard decisions to make, so start small so you can get used to the feeling of letting go.

When setting new boundaries think 'not too loose, not too tight'. Always give young people enough rope to explore the world and not enough to hang themselves. Sometimes it helps to ask yourself: what is the worst thing that can happen? Other times it helps to trial their new ideas with the proviso that you can adjust it if you feel it is not working. If they can live and learn from the consequences then everyone has won.

Keeping the home as stable as you can during these years is important, as well as trying to remain accessible to them as a parent. Young people will be experiencing a flood of new things so they will want to share the highs and lows with someone. Try not to lose family traditions amongst the change in pace and routine. They need some solid anchors around their new-found freedom. Parents need to be looking for new and interesting ways to connect and spend quality time together.

Please, don't stop being their parent just because they turn 18. When it comes to the really important decisions in life they still need your support and input. Arguments are an inevitable part of any relationship so don't be afraid to tackle the tough topics with them if you feel you need to. It's okay to disagree. It's okay to have a difference of opinion. What's important is that you respect their adult status as well as care.

Relationship is the Ultimate Answer

All the rules in the world will only backfire on you if you don't have a genuine relationship with your daughter. Mums and dads, this includes both of you. Dads, please don't just leave this one to the ladies no matter how awkward or difficult relating to your daughter starts to become once she hits puberty. You have to have a strong relationship with a daughter *before* you tell her what to do, because rules without relationship will only breed rebellion. Proven love is the only base which enables you to be the parent and hold a teenager accountable for their actions.

When I talk about having a relationship with your teenager, I don't mean being their friend. They have enough friends. Girls crave the unique connection that only a parent can offer. Moments of connection can happen anywhere, at any time. They don't have to be a big planned event for them to be meaningful. Whether big or small, they all form memories that last forever. We might remember connecting with mum late at night before we went to bed, or connecting with dad when he took us to cricket or at a beach holiday. It's amazing the times of connection that our memory retains.

I watch dads who deliberately invest into their daughters when they reach puberty and it pays off incredibly. Dads who coach their daughter's sports team become their hero. Building props for musical theatre, helping with a sausage sizzle fundraiser, selling tickets at the door, selling chocolates at work – there are so many ways you can help and play a part in your daughter's life. Dads, if you identify your girl's strengths and simply get involved in them, you will be irreplaceable in your girl's life.
One of my favourite sayings is *time poor = poor parenting*. I always like to get parents to acknowledge how time consuming

parenting is so they realistically and intentionally create space in their schedule to parent. Remember too that the more conflict you have with your daughter (and there will be times when conflict will be more intense than others) the more important it is to find positive moments of connection. Parenting through difficult times is a full-time job.

While this all sounds good in theory, I often find myself saying, "Where can I find the time? Someone has to pay the bills, clean the house and drive the kids around. Everything feels like it's just go, go, go. There is no time to stop and smell the roses. I don't even grow roses. I grow drought resistant plants, which don't require any of my attention. I have enough to take care of!"

I notice some families have a 'Family Planner' on their fridge which is used to co-ordinate everyone's comings and goings. Trying to read it is like trying to read the comings and goings of Grand Central train station. There are dance classes, sleepovers, date nights and music concerts overlapping and interconnecting. I personally laugh when I book in my grocery shopping at 8.30pm at night. How on earth did mothers cope when the shops shut at 5pm?

Sometimes I wonder what would happen if we just all stopped. If we just said, "You know what, this weekend I am not going to drive you anywhere. We aren't going out. We are just going to stay home and spend time together doing nothing." Besides World War III breaking loose because everyone wouldn't be getting their own way, I wonder if it would give us some time to stop and enjoy the simple things in life that we rush past each day.

We personally have to do this as a family to survive. It takes forethought and being prepared to say 'no' to things we'd like to attend, but we need to make our family a priority, especially as our children get older and their schedules also get fuller. As a mum I want to keep asking my young adult children to make time for family dinners and family beach days amongst their university and work schedules. Togetherness is everything.

STRATEGY 1:

10 Second Rule

If you want the end result - that is, socks picked up and the dishwasher unpacked with minimal fuss, then this is my advice. Pick your battle carefully and then keep your requests *short and simple.* Let me explain...

If you can't state your request in 10 seconds or less then chances are you won't get what you need from your daughter. The reason why you can't get things done could be as simple as you are using too many words. You could simply be negotiating and discussing things too much. If you converse for longer than 10 seconds about anything chances are the stakes will swing in your daughter's favour. Mums, this is especially true when it comes to us. We tend to over talk things (and attach way too much emotion to our words)!

Parents often think that using more words will give them a higher chance of winning their daughter over. Unfortunately not! When too many words are exchanged, parents often get dragged into long-winded debates with their children. By explaining the why and why nots of their requests, they give their girls ammunition to argue and manipulate with. In turn parents get worn down and give in.

One thing that railroads parents' requests every time is when they talk to their daughter about their personal needs and feelings. They might say to their daughter, "I want you to understand how much this is affecting me" ; or "You need to know how tired I am right now." This is a BIG mistake, which is about to side-track your request. Teenagers barely understand that their parents have feelings, let alone care about those feelings. They also smell their parents' fear and have been known to use it against them. Harsh but true!

Let me give you some 10-second examples...

Say: *I need you to put that phone down in the next five minutes and have a shower. I know you'd like to keep playing that game but you need to stop now and get ready for bed.*

Say: *It is 9 o'clock and that means you need to get ready for school. In the next ad break go and pack your lunch and get your uniform ready.*

No more words.

What do you do when they don't move? The reality is that this strategy is never going to get you results unless you use it in conjunction with other strategies in this chapter - so stay tuned.

Mums Write In...

In my house my husband and I have a secret personal buzzer system we use, just between the both of us. Once I have ranted for five minutes I buzz my own buzzer and remind myself, "That's probably enough, Sue." If I hit the 10-minute mark I tell my husband to shut me up with a little nod. If I hit the 15 minutes mark he can shut me up anyway he can. He can buzz the buzzer loud and clear! He usually stands behind the child I am lecturing and pretends to hang himself humorously... well it works in our household. I give myself ten minutes. My goodness Michelle, you are giving me ten seconds. My husband is going to LOVE this strategy. He has been trying to get me to shut up for ages!

STRATEGY 2:

Soft and Close

If you want a bad reaction out of a teenager, try bossing them around or yelling at them from the other side of the house. It's like waving a red flag in front of a bull. A better method is soft and close, which simply means speaking to them gently, on their level. Try standing or sitting next to them side-by-side, making your request politely and kindly. Using manners doesn't diminish your authority as a parent.

If things are really tense between you and your daughter, go one step further. Spend the first minute (60 whole seconds of your life) side-by-side, interested in what she is doing. It may feel like the longest 60 seconds of your life because chances are you will be in a hurry. Even so, I challenge you to delay your agenda and invest time in being interested in what she is doing BEFORE you request something from her.

A simple rule of thumb is this: for best results, speak to your teenager in the same way that you would like your teenager to speak to you.

Mums Write In...

I really focussed on this strategy today Michelle. My relationship with my daughter has been really tense over the last year or so. She is angry all the time and up and down constantly with friends. I'm sick of her taking it out on us. She's over sensitive at home and nothing I do or say is ever taken the right way. I find myself impatient and snappy, often in anticipation of her snapping at me. I have tended to bark instructions at her. I know my tone isn't always great. Today I went into her room and I just spent a moment with her before I asked her to come out and help me with the dinner. I can't say it magically worked, but I can see your point. I need to make a habit of slowing down and being in the moment with her. I'm taking this one on board.

STRATEGY 3:

Tip the Scales in Their Favour

I have heard professionals say that it is NEVER a good idea to take an iPhone off a child as a means of punishment because you run the risk of isolating them from their social circle and driving them underground. I'd actually like to use this statement as a way of highlighting the difference between punishment and discipline.

In my opinion, there are some times when it is quite appropriate for a parent to reduce social contact by taking a phone or saying 'no' to a social outing. However, I agree this shouldn't be a form of punishment. My basic premise for this is that I don't agree with the concept of punishment in the sense of needing to hurt a child to win a power struggle or modify behaviour. That is something I would never want to do to my child.

Our children are not lab rats or puppets. They are far more complex creatures than that. Although they are influenced by rewards and punishments, I hate the thought of my kids thinking that their life is a series of tit for tat reactions. Yes every action has a reaction, but entering into a tug of war with teenagers means that no-one wins. What we do to them, they are likely to spitefully do back to us, and it goes on and on.

Winning a fight by hurting or punishing a child means no one wins. Being a mean-spirited parent doesn't work. You can win an argument at work or on the rugby field with a little push and shove and possibly get away with it, but when you do it at home no one walks away a winner. You might temporarily get your own way, but in the end you lose the relationship.

There is no doubt there are times when it is important to win conflicts at home. However it is HOW we win those conflicts that make all the difference. I would prefer to win through consistent love and discipline rather than punishment. Discipline implies you need to bring stronger routine into a child's life to enable them to grow in a healthy way. Discipline teaches.

Just say your daughter was caught sleeping with her phone under her pillow, which she knows she is not allowed to do. Punishment approaches the situation like this:
You didn't do what I told you to do so you are going to be punished. I am going to take your phone off you.

I guarantee World War III.

Discipline approaches the situation like this:
I understand how tempting it would be to do that. I probably would have done that if I were 13. I need to bring better routine into your life right now. Things are getting a big crazy for you and that phone. I am going to take it for a few days to give your head a chance to clear. After two days we are going to bring the phone back but with some different conditions. I am doing this because I love you. I wouldn't bother if I didn't.

I guarantee World War III. I also guarantee she will respect you more.

I personally don't see any problem with this form of discipline.

In those two days I would suggest increasing relationship time with your daughter. During this time help her rebalance and ground her life on those things that matter the most. Sometimes we need to deliberately rebalance a child's life so they can regroup and grow in a healthy way. I call that discipline.

I hope these visuals help you understand the premise behind discipline, and self-discipline. I also hope they help you understand when to step in to your child's world and when not to. Here are my thoughts that I have shared over and over with families in my office.

If the scales are tipped in the wrong direction and the negatives are dominant in your daughter's life, she may need a bit more adult intervention (discipline) in order to rebalance things. Every time the negatives start outweighing the positives, our girls lose the ability to think straight and make healthy choices. Discipline rebalances the see saw so our daughters can take control of their lives again. To do this, parents need to win power struggles, minimise negative influences and say strong 'no's'. They may also need to introduce more positives.

If the scales are tipped in the right direction and the negatives are a small and manageable part of your daughter's life, parents can afford to back off a bit. Our daughters are likely to be able to manage things themselves and make positive choices. All they have to do is keep feeding the positives in their lives and keep an eye on the negative influences, which can accumulate quickly.

As our daughters grow into young adults we can no longer hand out discipline in order to rebalance or modify their behaviour. We can make suggestions but we have to allow them to learn to regulate themselves. It can be hard watching an 18-year-old struggle with the self-awareness to set their own boundaries in life. A hands-off approach can be frustrating and concerning, especially when they are sleeping in and skipping university. But take heart mums and dads, it's hard swinging in the air and they will eventually learn to ride the seesaw if we allow life to teach them.

Mums Write In...

Punishment doesn't work at all for my 15-year-old. She has absolutely no care or concern when I issue consequences (which I have just read should be called discipline!). Regardless of what we try we just can't get her to follow the rules at home. We are at our wits end! Everyone in the house is sick of it. I am at a total loss as to how to be effective in training her, as she doesn't seem to care. I could take everything off her and nothing would make any difference. Like you are saying here I find that it just adds to the negatives she feels she is facing. This strategy has really helped me understand that it's all about tipping the scales in her favour first. I can't discipline her before I do that. I actually think she doesn't have enough positives in her life right now and we wonder if she is depressed. Whatever I do I have to help keep her positive. Sometimes that is saying 'no' and sometimes that is making sure she does connect with things that bring her joy. It's a hard balance.

STRATEGY 4:

Piece by Piece

To effectively say 'no' or 'stop that' to a teenager all you have to do is talk less and do more. If you ask your daughter to do something and you don't get a response politely ask one more time. Everyone deserves a second chance. If you still don't get a response, don't keep asking. That will only make you look desperate. Instead talk less and do more.

Like Dr Phil says, "You teach people how to treat you." That includes your daughter. Teenagers, much like adults, just don't hear the word 'no' if it is said in isolation. It must be accompanied with an action. Think of it like this: if the police simply asked people to stop speeding I highly doubt they would get results. That is what speeding fines are for.

There is nothing wrong with a good old-fashioned consequence. In fact, if you issue the right kind of consequence it will actually help motivate your daughter in the right direction. However finding the right consequence is critical but FAR more difficult than it looks. Just remember that what your daughter was emotionally attached to when she was eight isn't likely to have the same impact today. A consequence has to make your daughter stop, stand up and take note!

The only thing I suggest you really try not to take away is the key positives in your daughter's life. This will only interrupt her life balance (Chapter 1: Disrespect - Strategy 3) and may end up being counterproductive. Our girls need positives as much as they need the air they breathe. A consequence should ideally chop off the excess or unnecessary elements in your daughter's life. I know that it might be tempting to touch your daughter's gymnastics, ballet and piano lessons, especially if she really enjoys them, but I encourage you to get more creative! Some families have told me they have literally had to buy their daughter something just so they can take it away!

However, in some situations it is impossible to avoid touching those core positive activities for a short amount of time. I was recently asked by a single mother to comment on whether she was being too hard on her 12-year-old daughter. Her daughter had been caught lying about her homework on several occasions across a number of weeks. The situation would always play out like this....

Her mother would come into her daughter's room mid-week and notice she would quickly minimise her computer screen. She would then ask her daughter, "What were you just doing on the computer?" Her daughter would reply, "I was doing my homework." Yet on Sunday night her mother would find out that her homework wasn't done, which would lead her to discover she had in fact been playing computer games during the week. She talked and talked to her daughter about lying and how disappointing her behaviour was, but nothing changed. Nothing!

Her daughter played netball, which her mother knew meant a lot to her. In fact it was literally the only thing she looked forward to. This mother had decided to tell her daughter that she would not be prepared to allow her to attend the game and training that week because she had lied to her. As much as her mother didn't want to take this experience away from her daughter she knew that missing out for one week would not damage her life. This mother's rationale was simple: I need to establish my authority now before things get out of hand. If I come in hard and fast, before my daughter gets any older, I may have a chance. I had to back her up even though I'm not a huge fan of taking away positive experiences in a teenager's life. I recognised that in this case it was the logical and most effective choice. She had to be the parent.

While consequences sound good in theory, I find they work best for those who have ample positives in their lives to start with. Those who struggle with depression, who don't have a strong social circle or who are extremely stubborn may not respond well to this strategy. Parents of those teenagers usually don't want to take many more positives away from them, they want to add them!

Some commonly used consequences include:

- phone time
- curfews
- television time
- social time
- time you are prepared to drive them places
- phone credit
- extra pocket money for that week
- money you are prepared to spend on extra curricular activities
- money you are prepared to spend on clothes or make up
- I am sure you have lots more ideas...

For low level, every day issues, try a piece-by-piece approach to issuing consequences. For example, you could say, "If you don't get up right now you won't be going to Emily's party." Once you have said that you have played all your cards. If she doesn't move you have no more ammunition left!

Piece by piece consequences says, "For every 15 minutes that dishwasher isn't unpacked I will pick you up fifteen minutes early from Emily's party. If it isn't unpacked in two hours you won't be going at all." As the minutes pass, our daughters are more likely to slow down and think about what they should be doing and the consequences associated with it. It's true, some will get stubborn and dig their heels in and refuse to respond. Some will learn easier than others.

Another example:
Say in 10 seconds or less (soft and close): "I need you to put that phone down in the next five minutes and have a shower. I know you'd like to keep playing that game but you need to stop now and get ready for bed."

They don't move (surprise, surprise).

Talk less. Do more.

Say in 10 seconds or less (soft and close): "For every 10 minutes you aren't in the shower I will be putting that phone away for another half an hour after dinner tomorrow night. If you aren't in the shower in one hour you won't be on that phone at all tomorrow night. Your choice! I am not going to speak to you again."

Talk less. Do more. Walk off.

I guarantee you will only have to follow through once and next time you speak you will get some more movement.

Mums Write In...

I am hearing you, but it's such hard work and sometimes it just doesn't work, no matter how hard you try. The other day I rang her to ask her to hang out this washing. Simple job I thought. This was met with disgruntled sighs and I could 'feel the eye rolls' over the phone! I explained that it was actually HER washing in the machine and could she please hang it out. She informed me that she really shouldn't have to seeing as though she was on holidays!! So I said, "Okay, then by your standards when I'M on holidays I don't need to do ANYTHING – e.g. no cooking, shopping etc." She told me she would do it but asked that it be noted she "wasn't happy about it". I told her that I would call back in ten and for every ten minutes it wasn't done it would be ten minutes she would have to wait for me to drive her to her friends on the weekend. For the record ... she didn't hang it out as it looked like it might rain (which it didn't!)

STRATEGY 5:

Pay Back Jobs

Recently a beautiful mother wrote to me for some advice. Her daughter had been grounded - for good reason. She desperately wanted to attend the 'school encouraged' social, which all her friends were attending. It was the highlight of the school year. The dilemma was, does her mum back down and let her go, or not?

I put the question to our Facebook community, who weighed in with a variety of responses, including:

- A grounding is a grounding so don't budge.
- The punishment has to fit the crime so it depends what she did wrong.
- School socials come once in a lifetime, so let her go.
- Trade the grounding for another punishment.

I get all sorts of questions about whether a punishment, once set, can be negotiated. Surely once parents say something they then have to follow through in the same way a policeman does with the letter of the law?

I am of the opinion that parents can change their mind and still remain credible especially if it happens sparingly. Be consistent with discipline, yes, but don't be restricted. Discipline has to make kids do the math but not make them drown in the math. Use your common sense as a parent. That being said, there are times where negotiation just won't work.

Never negotiate with terrorists. Only negotiate when young people come to you in a spirit of good will.

Tonight, I spoke to a father who was very concerned about his daughter's gaming habits. She was online every waking moment of every day, to the point that she wasn't socialising or coming out of her room. When her parents would turn the internet off to allow her to have a break she would lose her temper. The girl would get so mad that she would refuse to eat until they turned the internet back on. This would last for days until her parents caved in. Sounds like they are being held to ransom to me. I wouldn't negotiate in a situation like this.

To Get Ungrounded You Must Earn 50 Points

Choose from the following jobs	YES	NO
Hug your mum like you mean it = 5 points		
Empty dishwasher = 5 points		
Prepare and cook dinner = 10 points		
Clean toilets = 10 points		
Wash back deck = 10 points		
Buy some flowers for your mother = 10 points		
Mow lawn = 20 points		
Wash kitchen chairs = 20 points		
Wash the showers = 20 points		
Vacuum the whole house = 20 points		
Read a book and write a summary of it = 20 points		
Wash all windows outside = 50 points		
TOTAL POINTS =		

One method I have seen work well is pay back jobs. If your daughter has been given a punishment, which in the light of day seems a little harsh, why not use a negotiation tool called 'payback jobs'. Give them the opportunity to pay back or swap the original punishment by doing set jobs. You might provide them with a list of possible jobs and ask them to choose 50 points worth in order to earn back their privileges. I always, always suggest that a decent, heartfelt apology should precede any pay back jobs. I will say it again - never negotiate with terrorists. There is nothing cool about being held hostage by a 14 year-old.

Mums Write In...

Last year we had an incident with the phone bill. What parent of a teenage girl hasn't been caught – it's just the $$$ value that varies! In one month our home phone was used for MANY calls to mobiles and our daughter somehow managed to find enough time in her days to send over 1,800 text messages (try explaining to a 13-year-old that a text message costs 25c whether it says 'K', 'KK' or the entire 160 characters!). All of this led to more than $1,000 in phone bills in one month (I try not to dwell on the clothes, shoes, food or electricity bills I could have used this money for). For a few months prior to this our phone bills were creeping up and our daughter had been warned several times about excessive phone calls, mobiles for emergency use only blah blah blah, so this was the final straw... GROUNDED UNTIL THE $1,000 PHONE BILL REPAID! She missed the school dance that EVERYONE was going to and I drew up a payment plan with jobs and corresponding amounts (eg $2.50 to clean the toilet, $10 to wash the car etc ... I even incorporated some penalties – bad attitude minus $1 etc). We had hoped that the thought of missing out on activities with her friends would motivate her to get in and get it over and done with... WRONG! The amount she had to earn seemed so insurmountable to her that she couldn't see how she would ever get through it all, so why bother even trying? Weeks rolled past and she had *done very little. She had missed a few social activities but just couldn't seem to get it together. We were generous in the $$$ we paid for chores done, gave extra $$$ for a good report card and made a few other ex-gratia payments along the way but were determined not to let her off the hook. It was actually our daughter who approached us to renegotiate the terms of our arrangement. She suggested that for every $100 she repaid, she could have an outing/ friends over etc. We agreed to this and it was amazing to see the peaks and troughs in her motivation depending on what social activity was approaching. Eventually the $1,000 was repaid and we all learnt some lessons from that experience. We also locked down our phones and made sure this couldn't happen again. It was a torturous few months for all concerned but I think we came out the other side feeling our daughter had learnt something - not the least of which was the value of a dollar and that we meant business when we handed down a sentence. In the future I will carefully consider the punishment I hand out because you have to be able to enforce it and see it through, and I think it's important to be reasonable and flexible in your terms – after all, even the Department of Transport allows you to pay off your speeding fine in instalments!*

STRATEGY 6:

Make Room for PE Uniforms

Be prepared to utilise the incidental opportunities that life presents in order to teach your teenager how to respect you, your time, your money and your things. You have to seize the moment - 'carpe diem' as one might say. Sometimes life isn't black and white and there is a compromise and a life lesson to be learnt.

A counsellor I know and have a great deal of respect for often shares these words with me: "When parents don't respect themselves they may always feel like their teenager doesn't respect them." It's a mirror of how they see themselves. People will only respect us to the degree we respect ourselves. We teach people how we want them to treat us." I think she is right.

Small incidental lessons like the one I am about to share with you are powerful ways of teaching your teenagers respect. Any instances where you are in the 'driver's seat' are moments you can use to your advantage.

Here's a great little example that shows how easy it is to teach your children that your time is valuable...

Daughter's text: I forgot my PE uniform and I really, really need it before my class this afternoon or I'll be in big trouble. Please, please bring it and meet me at the office at lunchtime.

Mum's text: What's in it for me? You are interrupting my afternoon.

Daughter's text: ummmm....

Mum's text: I need the washing done tonight – three loads and hung out.

Daughter's text: Okay I'll do it tonight.

Mum's text: Deal.

Mum then drove up to the school and took the uniform to the office. Instead of feeling resentful for having to bring the uniform up or feeling guilty because her kid was the one who forgot it she proudly said to the school receptionist, "I'm getting the washing done tonight for bringing this up!"

The receptionist responded, "Good on you! You would not believe how many mothers come up here and say, 'Oh it's my fault she didn't remember it. I really should have reminded her this morning. I know she's got lots to remember on Tuesdays.' Like a 16 year-old can't remember to bring their PE uniform to school!"

Teenagers need a reason to show respect. Unfortunately, they won't often voluntarily respect your time, money or wishes without a reason! You have to give them a reason to show you respect. You have to teach them how to treat you.

Mums Write In...

I had a light bulb moment after reading this! My daughter rang and she wanted me to pick her up early from work which was going to inconvenience me because I was knee deep in folding the family's washing and I wanted - no NEEDED - to get it done. Instead of rushing out the door in a frenzy (like I usually do) and then apologising that I didn't get there fast enough I made her wait. I folded HER school socks first! She was only waiting for like 10 – 15 minutes but she had to wait nonetheless and when she complained (like I knew she would) and texted me 100 times in the 10 minutes that I was on my way I explained to her that I was busy and I had things to do too. My time was important too. I seized the moment thanks to your advice and let her know that it was my car and my petrol and my time she was demanding. Next time she rings to be picked up early she might say please. And I might get a coffee on the way!

STRATEGY 7:

Unlimited Confidence

So they did the wrong thing. They stuffed up. It will happen. You can either come down hard on them (exactly like they are expecting) or you can try another tactic. Don't get me wrong. There are times when coming down hard is the appropriate thing to do, especially when her safety is involved. However, I have also found that there are other times when that is not the best strategy to use. Mixing it up a bit can be very effective!

Having unlimited confidence in your daughter is so important. If you were to say to your daughter, "You are better than this..."; or "I know this doesn't represent who you really are..." ; or "You aren't acting like yourself right now..." It then gives room for a strong rebound.

Shaming is never the best platform to move things forward, especially when a girl's spirits are low! Affirming and believing the best in our girls, even when they are at their worst, is critical. Before addressing your daughter's failures think carefully about how you want to approach her. If you encourage her chances are she will rise to meet your expectations. After all we often get what we expect in life. Your daughter's confidence starts with your confidence in her.

Mums Write In...

This made me think of the time that I didn't take my daughter's iPhone off her. I could have but I didn't. I decided that taking her phone off her was not the right decision. By taking away her phone, it would have been taking away her connection to friends. I said to her, "I could have taken your phone off you and you know that, don't you?" She dropped her head and agreed. "But what I am going to say to you is that this is not what I am going to do." Her head raises and her eyes meet mine. Silence. "We both know that what you did was wrong but what I want you to know is that you are responsible for your actions and as a young woman who is still learning right from wrong, you need to understand that we are going to come to an agreement. I know how important you feel your phone is to you and you want to be seen as being responsible and for me to not treat you as a little kid." She agreed. "Well we are going to take an adult approach. You are stronger and better than this." I still gave her some other consequences but not to do with her phone. This worked, as the alternatives were still enough for her to learn, without the feeling of totally losing control of her life. And let's face it, their phones are their lives! Basically taking away the phone was not part of the consequence - there are other means of teaching kids and the punishment needs to fit the crime.

STRATEGY 8:

Go Halves

So really, money doesn't grow on trees?! Who would have thought? That's a harsher reality than the discovery that Santa and the Easter Bunny aren't real. In our consumer society I know that every family battles to teach their girls the value of money. Here is a short list of other ideas which I have seen work fairly successfully. By 'fairly successfully' I mean just that: fairly successfully. That's all I can promise here.

Give your daughter a set amount of money each week and expect her to manage her own purchases including entertainment and take away food. This will force to her make conscious choices and set priorities.

Expect them to get a part time job. Or if you prefer your teenager to earn money at home, but are tired of arguing about jobs, why not outsource them? Why not get them to do jobs for neighbours or other family members? This is my personal favourite strategy because it allows someone else to monitor how hard they are working, not you! They are more likely to work hard for someone they are less familiar with.

If you are giving out pocket money, only pay them for doing additional jobs that go beyond the call of duty. Why on earth would you pay them to put out the garbage when you have to do it for free? Agree about the jobs they need to do in order to contribute to the home and be a part of the family, then add jobs they can choose to do to earn money. If they are pre-teens they might find it fun to submit an invoice each Friday and get paid.

For everything new your teenager buys ask them to give away or sell something that they no longer wear or use. Our teenagers' cupboards are usually jam packed with stuff that is going to waste and they don't value. Not only does this strategy help them keep their rooms a little more organised but it also gives them a sense of resourcefulness and responsibility to do something with what they have. Who knows, they may realise that their old things might be worth something after all.

'I'll go you halves strategy! It is amazing how quickly teenagers don't need something when they have to part with their cash to pay for half of it. They do think a lot harder and for a lot longer if they have to part with their money as well as yours.

Don't buy things the same day they request it. Let them think about it and make sure they really want it. Try the 'yes you can have it but you can't have it now' strategy. It does mean you have to have time to go back to the shop, which can be annoying! I am reminded of Oprah's advice years ago: "Freeze your credit card and if you really need it you will be able to defrost it and use it a few days later."

Choose a dollar figure and tell your daughter that you won't buy anything over that amount on that day.

Get parents' wages out in cash for the fortnight and literally show your teenagers where the money goes each week.

Mums Write In...

I often find the option of 'going halves' is a good one too – it helps my image of 'reasonable and generous parent' (who can argue with that) but reinforces the need for the child and teen to be responsible and committed to the item / activity. It's hard sometimes though. My daughter spent about four months with a cracked iPod screen because she couldn't (actually wouldn't) get the $40 she needed for her half of the repair – it drove me insane and the glass crumbled and threatened the feet of all who walked in our house – I don't know how she could even read the screen but I guess most of what's said on Facebook (the iPod's primary use) is pretty predictable (to me anyway!!) I totally laugh when my kids tell me how BUSY they are working (a part time job!) and that is why they can't help around the house!!! And I don't work?! When I tell them I am too busy working to cook tea tonight they look at me like I'm the laziest thing to ever hit the planet.

CHAPTER TWO

Social Media

A Snap Shot of Reality

The amount of time 8 to 18-year-olds spend watching TV, playing video games or surfing the internet has increased dramatically to around 7.5 hours a day[18]. That is 53 hours a week. They spend more time in front of a screen per day than they do exercising in an entire week[19].

82% of teenagers use social media, with the most common services used being Facebook, YouTube, Instagram, Snapchat and Skype[20].

The average teenage girl sends 4050 texts per month[21]. That is more than six texts per waking hour!

On average, teenagers have three social media accounts[22].

Only 61% of kids and teenagers who use social media have their main account set to private[23].

45% of kids and teenagers who use social media report that they received nasty comments, while 36% report that they have been exposed to inappropriate or hurtful content[24].

19% of teenagers report having been cyberbullied in the last 12 months[25].

Three quarters of Australian kids are accidentally exposed to pornography before the age of 17[26].

49% of young people have sent a sexually suggestive image, and 67% of young people have received a sexually suggestive image[27].

9% of teenagers say they have been contacted by a stranger online in the last 12 months[28].

A Generation Left Behind

Let's face it. Most of us parents are like the rest of us... left behind. I regularly watch my four year-old niece effortlessly pick up my sister's phone and take photos of herself, find her favourite photo of herself, play games and pretend to answer text messages. How is her mother going to be able to keep up with her in ten years' time? And who taught her how to work that thing anyway?

It feels like yesterday that we were using a hand held phone (with a cord), playing cassette tapes and typing on a typewriter (with blot out ink). Then came the explosion of technology that has changed the world at lighting speeds that we are all scrambling to keep up with. These days I can't fathom a world without the internet or my phone but as a teenager I wasn't so dependent on it. Technology was cool but not that cool. We had Donkey Kong and Parachute. Cool, but not cool enough to keep me glued to a computer screen all day.

It's important that we stop and see things from this generation's perspective for a minute. They were born into a world of technology. They have never been without it. It is their normal. They have always been able to Google their name, spell check their assignments and reach their friends 24/7. Their online world is constant and instant. Social decisions are made in the moment through group chats. They don't pre-plan weeks in advance. They don't have to.

A client was telling me that her daughter no longer leaves the house in order to watch a movie with her girlfriends. Instead they all watch the movie simultaneously in their own bedrooms and socialise together in a group chat during the movie. They don't even have to pay for popcorn. All they need in life can be found in technology and their lives are entwined with it. And as I write this book I am aware that within 12 months, this is going to sound old school.

The link between social media and identity is unique to this generation. 'You don't exist if you're not online' is a phrase that we as adults have heard but have struggled to understand. Young people are deeply and emotionally connected to technology. It represents them. Social media delves into a personal realm of our lives, which I'm sure that none of us ever thought possible when we laid eyes on our first computer.

Girls who don't have their own phone often get excluded from social invitations. No one wants to make a phone call or text someone's mother. There is only one way to communicate these days and that is online. It is no wonder that teenagers don't feel like they are a complete person who has a complete social life unless they are online.

This may explain why all hell breaks loose when you take social media away from young people. You are in effect deleting them. It is erasing who they are and a very real aspect of their world. That means that the horrible social media account that you want to shut down isn't just a social media account; it is their identity. It is who they are when they aren't who they are.

However, there is no doubt in my mind that amongst all the influences that teenagers have in their lives the single most dangerous influence lives in their back pockets. If you could see what I see on a daily basis I guarantee you would see technology differently.

I do hear the worst stories that would make anyone's hair stand on end. That being said, when it comes to social media, the worst things don't necessarily happen to the worst families. The challenges that are associated with social media can reach anyone, anytime. No one is exempt. You don't have to have a bad kid for them to get into serious trouble. I have had so many strong, committed families in my office with serious issues relating to social media.

This is the worst story I have been involved in. A mother went into her 15-year-old daughter's room in the morning before school, looking for her glasses. Her daughter was sitting on the end of her bed with earphones in her ears, back towards her mother. Mum tapped her on the shoulder to get her attention but as she did, she noticed the bed sheets move. With some concern she quickly pulled back the covers and found a 40-year-old man in her daughter's bed. He had been let in the house by her daughter through the night! They had met online months earlier, struck up a relationship and there he was.... in her bed. The quick-thinking mum tried to get a photo of him as he fled the house, but he covered his face. Five police were at the scene within minutes but they didn't catch him in time.

A more common scenario, but equally as scary, is this one. A young girl I work with sent a nude image to a boy she liked. She regretted it almost immediately and asked him to delete it. He told her that he did and the two never spoke of the incident again. The girl moved schools and she quickly put it behind her. Twelve months later the boy was playing football with some boys from her new school. Her name came up in conversation. The boy pulled up the image (which had never been deleted) and within 24 hours almost everyone in her grade had received a copy of the photo. Twelve months later!!!

A teenager's online life comes with a range of new risks, some which parents understand and some which parents don't understand. These risks are easy for young people to take in the comfort of their own home where they feel safe. They can happen far quicker than any risk we took as teenagers and they require far less planning. Within seconds young people can be interacting with unsafe people or content without their parents knowing.

I have seen young people (GOOD young people) talking to paedophiles on an iPod while they are talking to their mum who is making a Sunday roast. I have seen 18-year-old girls come to my office with pornography addictions that started when they were 13, while exchanging photos with their boyfriend. I have seen them addicted to gaming and become so aggressive and manipulative that their mothers are scared to be alone with them. I have seen girls become obsessed with body shape and size after feeding on a steady diet of 'thinspiration'. It started with the phone!

On a less intense note, mums tell me that although their daughters may not be sending nude images or talking to paedophiles, they are constantly distracted and disengaged. They are not paying enough time to their schoolwork, family time or day-to-day jobs. It's like this generation is in a relationship with their phones instead of being in relationship with the people who love them. They are not present in their actual lives.

Our daughters have a love-hate relationship with their phones. They can't live happily with them but they also can't live without them. They admit to being addicted. That is why they need us (rather than want us) involved in their online world. Without us it is highly possible they could lose their way.

We all like to think we are bringing up our kids but if we are realistic their greatest influence lives in their back pockets. To ask parents to stay up to date with every new app that comes along is too much to ask, but to ask them to stay aware is fathomable. We have to be aware of what technology is coming into our home and what that technology has the potential to do. We have to be aware of how our teenagers are using that technology. Educated is awesome if it's possible but aware, eyes wide open aware, is adequate. Aware is my aim.

It's Not When - It's How

The issue of supervising your daughter online is a serious one, especially in the primary and middle school years. Too often children receive their first electronic devices with little or no guidance leaving them vulnerable to an adult world. That being said, supervising a girl's online life is in reality, easier said than done.

Too often our daughters see their online world as their own private world that their parents have no right to be a part of. When our daughters hold this belief, not only do they take uncalculated risks, it makes them more vulnerable to issues relating to paedophiles, sexting, pornography and cyber bullying. Young people who want privacy online aren't necessarily behaving poorly; they are often just protecting their identity and their friend's identity.

Most parents I know are faced with decisions about social media when their daughters are very young - usually between ages 10 and 12. For some, the pressure to be online comes much younger than this. Those with older brothers or sisters often get online so early that by the time they are 13 they are well and truly immersed in the world of social media.

When your teenager is 10, 11 or even 12 they are relatively easy to manage. It is therefore easy to say 'yes' to social media without spending a lot of time thinking about how you will manage it and what restrictions you might put on it. However put a few years on her and a few more hormones, the desire for a boyfriend and a few friends you aren't so keen on, and you may not say 'yes' so quickly. Your 'yes' may come with a few more conditions; conditions which are hard to administer later if they haven't been put in place from the beginning.

My argument is this.

When your daughter first comes to you and asks for a phone or a social media account stop and think about it. You might want to be cautious. You might want to think about how to set things up to get through the bumpiest years that may lie ahead. Remember once you give them the phone it is there for life. When it comes to phones (and social media accounts) I have one thought - Don't set rules WHEN there is a problem. Set rules BEFORE there is a problem.

There is always a lot of discussion about what is the right age to buy your child a phone or allow them access to social media. I don't think there is a right or wrong answer. There is no magical age that makes a phone safe. I have personally tried both - a later start with my eldest and an earlier start with my youngest. I see families make both options work well. Why? It is not just WHEN you allow your daughter on social media that matters. It is HOW you allow them on social media that is more important. The same goes for a phone. It is not WHEN you give them a phone that matters. It is HOW you give them a phone that is most important.

Over the years, as my experience and knowledge has grown, I have changed my thoughts as to when it is appropriate to allow young people on social media. I used to be quite a believer of holding off until they had the cognitive maturity to support their online decision and suggested parents wait until they were at least 13 (I actually suggested 14+). However these days I see great sense in getting in early and walking beside a child while they are still teachable.

There is a window of opportunity between 10 and 12-years-old, but once this window closes you have lost valuable teaching time that you can't get back. I am also not suggesting that children should have their own social media accounts without parent supervision or safety software. I am also not suggesting this is appropriate for all children or families. It is just something for you to consider.

Perhaps the answer is this: allow them a social media account, which by all merits is actually yours. You set it up including installing the software that enables you to receive messages that are sent and received (there are some great programs around these days). You spend time on it with her daily. Ask her questions like, "Are you sure you want to post that? Once you hit send you can't get it back. Are you happy for all your friends to see it or happy for someone to take a screen shot of it or send it on to someone else?" Help her think critically and use self-control. You can't always do this with a 13 to 14 year-old. They just aren't that teachable.

As your teenager grows, their maturity will hopefully grow with them allowing them greater autonomy and independence. In my experience, you have up until they are about 16 to manage social media. After that point your opportunity to set boundaries may have ended, so use the time wisely while you have it.

Don't Blame Social Media

The reality is that nothing will test your relationship with your daughter like social media will. Social media gives our teenagers an opportunity to rebel. It ticks all the boxes – it is an area that teenagers have power over their parents and it is easy for your daughter to exercise this power, especially when they have access to computers at school, shopping centres, coffee shops and friends' houses. The reality is you can't completely stop them anyway, which is what every parent wants to hear.

The truth is that teenagers *can* set up social media without your permission. Then there is the issue of being grounded from using the Internet at home, when they still have to use the computer for school... some grounding! Parents regularly tell me how frustrating it is to try and get their daughters' password from them when they want to shut down inappropriate social media accounts or add additional safety software. They often tell me that their daughter refuses to give it to them. I know that parents feel like they will probably go and set up another account in secret even if they relent and give them what they ask for.

'Break the rules like a pro' is a saying that sums up this generation online. In general I think young people get away with far too much online, which has the potential to surface in the years to come. As a result our daughters assume they can say and do whatever they like online and are surprised if there are consequences. The computer screen gives our girls an opportunity to become a different person, whether that person be someone more sexually mature or someone who is horribly mean.

If you have lost control you may be having conversations that sound like this...
Parent: Take down those photos.
Teenager: No.
Parent: I'll shut down your account.
Teenager: You can't. I'll just set up another one.
Parent: I will take your phone off you.
Teenager: Yeah right like that's going to stop me. I've got a school laptop!

You have to rely on your authority as a parent *and your relationship with your child* as a basis for navigating through social media. If you have lost control, the issue is about your parenting, not just social media. Don't blame social media. Social media is neither good nor bad. It's a challenge but if the challenge was not social media it would be something else.

You will always have to recognise there is a generation gap in the way you and your daughter think about technology. The only way to bridge that is through communication. Talk to your daughter about her online life regularly. I always encourage girls to have an accountability buddy who is closer to their age – someone who is in their early 20s whom they can be honest with about what is happening in their online life.

Give them age appropriate trust. One mother grounded her daughter from texting for a week and left the phone in her possession because she needed it for general communication with the family. She trusted her not to text during this time. "Are you serious?" I genuinely asked. "How did you know she didn't text?" "I just trusted her" was the answer! Get my point?

They are teenagers. Expect them to act like teenagers. Their whole mission is to have a life without you in it. Your job is to protect them, not to trust them. For goodness sake don't trust them in the same way you would trust a mature adult. What you can't trust is that they have the capacity to make adult-like decisions, especially under pressure.

Faulty Beliefs

Most wise adults understand the dynamics of being online. They have a belief system that supports their online choices. In turn they keep their relationship intact and their jobs secure! These are some of the basic things that guide sensible adults' online choices...

- The web is a public place.
- Nothing is private online.
- You are never anonymous.
- You always leave a digital footprint.
- Once you hit send you can't get it back or control where it goes.
- Your posting and comments can be found for years.
- Your digital reputation will impact future jobs and positions.
- People online are real people who are impacted by your actions.
- Nothing can be permanently deleted.

However when we talk to teenagers about internet reality they don't seem to get it. I sometimes feel like no one is home. How many times have I said, "Once you hit send you can't get it back" and they still hit the send button!!!! How many times have I given a cyber safety presentation in a high school only to find a girl has gone home and sent a nude on Snapchat that evening! This has forced me to think about what drives this behaviour and how to best counteract it.

Teenagers' beliefs drive their behaviour. Faulty beliefs drive risky online behaviour. Faulty beliefs like "I don't exist if I am not online"; "My online world is my own private world (that their parents have no right to be a part of)"; and "There are no real consequences online". All these beliefs have the potential to trip up our daughters if we are not attentive to them.

Without exception teenagers who get into trouble online hold one or more of these faulty beliefs. To guide our daughters we have to understand them and plug into what is going on inside their heads. I find that families are unconsciously supporting faulty beliefs by doing simple things like these:

Allowing young people to use phones 24/7 without ensuring adequate time outs. This reinforces that they don't exist if they are not online. If our daughters don't have time away from media they never find out they can exist without it.

Being too busy to check accounts and passwords. This reinforces that teenagers' online world is their own private world that parents shouldn't be a part of.

Turning a blind eye to poor online behaviour or not addressing issues like sexting. This reinforces that there are no real life consequences or rules associated with being online, and that the online world operates differently than in the real world.

We need to make sure we are educating our kids about internet reality through our parenting choices. If we don't understand, challenge and re-educate young people's faulty beliefs they will totally dictate the decisions they make online. We also have to know that what we do either reinforces or counteracts their beliefs about being online. Every single suggestion I make in this chapter is designed to deliberately challenge faulty beliefs and reinforce Internet reality.

STRATEGY 1:

Never a Gift

Our daughters consider a phone as necessary as the air they breathe. They expect us to provide one for them. However having a phone is a privilege, not a right.

If you buy your daughter a mobile phone (or phone plan) as a gift it is really difficult to take that gift back. After all she will argue that a gift is owned by the one who received it! That is why I suggest that parents own all technology in their home and give their children the privilege of using it if they use it responsibly. If the parent owns technology they are also free to install any safety software they feel necessary.

As our daughters get older they will gain more autonomy online. Take advantage of this strategy while you can because it will only work until your daughter is old enough to buy herself a phone and a phone plan and repair her own cracked phone screen!

Mums Write In...

I just now realise how naive I was when this whole thing started and would never have guessed it would become the monster it now is! I wish I'd have thought or known to put all or most of your rules/strategies in place in the early days. She was so keen for permission to get on social media that I think she'd have agreed to pretty much anything! Trying to bring in a new regime now gives me a headache and palpitations just thinking about it. And from a parent who didn't realise ... promise me that EVERY TIME you speak to parent groups PLEASE stress to all those pre-teen parents and technology virgins how important it is to implement tight guidelines from the absolute onset, even if they don't think their child needs it because she will. Maybe not at 13 but it won't be long!!

STRATEGY 2:

Crystal Clear Agreements

I think it is ridiculous to have a written agreement for everything that happens in a home. I am not personally great at keeping checklists or my kids' chores on whiteboards or charts. I prefer a bit of random chaos. But when it comes to social media a written contract really is essential. Nothing should be left unsaid.

I like to write phone and social media agreements with teenagers' input. Although you will always have to have the final word, the exercise is certainly an interesting one! It forces girls to communicate assumptions regarding their phone's use and express their ideas and disappointments upfront. It will also force parents to stop and think about whether their expectations are reasonable.

There is a lot of room for negotiation in the contract I have written below. This agreement is a conservative starting point for pre-teens that you can adjust to suit you. I encourage you to tailor make it for your family and base it on the age and needs of your child. For example, a 14 year-old is going to have far more autonomy online than outlined in this contract.

Try not to leave the agreement in a place where it will be lost and forgotten. Keep it in a visible place. This will be a good reminder for both you and your daughter that you are serious about following through. During the busyness of life there will be times when you stick to the contract and times when you neglect it. That is normal. At least a contract gives you something to come back to.

I also encourage parents to let their daughters know that the contract isn't a rigid representation of their relationship. Parents should be free to parent over and above the bounds of the contract, understanding that it is impossible to write down every scenario that might take place in their relationship.

Once you finalised your agreement you have two options as far as the management of it goes. You can either manage the agreement yourself, install software to help you, or rely on a combination of both. There are a range of software options for parents to consider at www.esafety.gov.au. I personally think it is next to impossible to manage phones without safety software in place. However if you are going to install software on their phones be upfront and honest with them about it.

Remember, too, as young people grow they do need greater autonomy online. Parents need to let go of the reins and give them their space. Please, please remember that safety software is only a part of the answer. You still need to have eyes in the back of your head because things can still go wrong and software is full of loopholes and glitches.

I sit with many parents who have already allowed their daughter to use social media without any guidelines. They feel like the 'horse has already bolted' and they have no hope of establishing new boundaries. It can be very difficult to pull in the reins when your teenager is used to having the freedom to use technology as they wish. If the thought of implementing this contract makes your stress levels rise I suggest you take things one step at a time. I meet many families who know their teenager needs stronger boundaries but feel that enforcing them may trigger major and irreparable conflict. If this is you, choose one boundary, like 'Shut down time at 10.00pm' ; or 'No sleeping with your phone in your room at night'. Start where you can.

Sample Contract

This is a sample agreement which has been negotiated between parents of a just turned 12 year-old girl who is relatively responsible online. It covers all the basics that a family needs to cover when it comes to a girl's online life.

Parents' Agreement

I will set up all technology to ensure your safety and enable homework to be done as a priority. Your entertainment is a secondary issue.
I own and manage all technology.
I will install safety software to protect you.
I will conduct random checks of your online activity.
I won't unnecessarily invade your privacy.
I will never embarrass you online.
There are certain things that I am concerned about. These things include sexual predators, identity theft, bullying, sexting and pornography. I would like to keep talking to you about these things because I know you may come across them.
I hope you will communicate with me if you are unsure about anything online. I will try never to over react if you tell me about a problem you are having online.

Teenagers' Agreement

My time on the internet will be between the hours of 8am and 8.30pm except for meal times and family activities when I may be asked to put the phone away.

All electronic devices including mobile phones will be shut down at 8.30pm at night and put in the office to recharge.

While online I will behave politely and show respect for others.

I will not share any personal details online including my name, address, phone number, sporting club or school.

I will not enter competitions to win free things nor will I buy things online from companies that ask for private information such as my birth date, address or bank details.

I will never click on links in emails or open attachments from people I don't know.

I will ask before downloading or installing games, music or videos.

I understand that I need to be cautious online.

I will never meet with anyone I have talked to online without getting my parent's permission.

I will let my parents know if I come across pornography.

I will not respond to requests for nudes and will speak to my parents immediately if this happens.

I will be cautious about the photos I post of my friends and myself.

I will talk to my parents if I ever feel uncomfortable or upset by something that happened online.

Signed ______________________________ (Parent)

Signed ______________________________ (Teenager)

Date to be reviewed: Every school term

Mums Write In...

Our family's biggest win in setting healthy boundaries was installing a modem. It creates a wifi stream the kids sign on to wifi with and we have an app that manages a schedule with three options: no wifi, homework mode (so no social media, Youtube, etc (you can block websites) or general. The wifi blocks adult content. Parents can be on a different wifi band. All websites are tracked so you can view history. Works for all devices using wifi so you can turn off internet to phones, Xbox etc overnight or during times in day. We also use an app that you can load on to each child's phone. Turning the schedule off turns games off as well. You can turn it on or off remotely and easily adjust the schedule. It really has saved our family!

STRATEGY 3:

Insist on Transparency

I want you to do something for me. I want you to directly ask your daughter to be completely transparent with you when it comes to her online life. I can already hear you hesitating. You just breathed in and you said to yourself, "Is that even possible? Do I have the right to ask her that?"

In the back of most parents' minds is the nagging, unsettling notion that our daughters can set up fake profiles and trick any safety software we install. We know that if we confiscate their phone it is possible that they can borrow their friend's spare phone or purchase a second-hand phone at school the next day. It scares us senseless so we waiver. We hesitate. We don't eyeball the topic.

Although this is true, I still believe we are doing our kids a disservice if we don't ask for transparency. When they go for job interviews in the future there will be little an employer is unable to uncover. Their digital footprint is real. That's why asking for transparency makes sense. It reinforces the fact that the Internet is a public place.

The trick is to ask for transparency CONFIDENTLY. Lay out your expectations *without flinching*. I promise that if you flinch, your daughter will see it. She can smell fear. I often laugh when mothers tell me, "I'm surprised she hasn't worked out that she can say no to me and I wouldn't be able to do anything about it." You might feel like you are bluffing your way through the management of social media but as they say, 'you have to be in it to win it'. Never, NEVER allow your kids to bully you out of their world!

Passwords are the trickiest things to keep a handle on. Try keeping a password list on the fridge (or somewhere else if siblings may be tempted to use them inappropriately) and expect your daughter to update them each time she changes them. For some reason teenagers constantly need to change their passwords. You can obviously use software to help manage this as well.

If your daughter does fully allow you into her online world, please be respectful of it. Don't jump on every little swear word and error she makes. Remember she talks to her friends all day long without you being over her shoulder and she does just fine. Please don't comment and get involved in her online conversations. That's just embarrassing. Be silent. Be discreet. Only bring to her attention things that are critical.

I encourage parents to literally schedule time into their diaries to thoroughly check their daughter's social media accounts. I would recommend scheduling this into your diary every month and at any time you are concerned about your daughter's online activity. I also encourage parents to Google their daughter's name occasionally. If parents don't schedule check-ups in their diary they often go by the wayside.

Mums Write In...

I worry about the possibility of pushing my daughter 'underground' if I pull the reins too tight. My friend's daughter got her phone taken off her and suddenly BOOM....there were magically five second hand phones around the house!!!!! I joined Instagram (under protest and after much resistance) shortly after she did purely so I could keep an eye on her as a 'friend'. She accepted my request but not too long after that I found she had set up another profile – no doubt to hide from me. I'm a 'friend' on that profile now too, but of course you can still be a 'friend' and yet be blocked from certain posts, etc. (I've been unfriended before and pulled the pin on her completely until the situation changed.) I would suggest random auditing of accounts as they are sure to delete questionable comments/conversations, etc, if they know when you're going to check it. I try to get my daughter to understand I have no desire to CATCH her doing anything wrong. I really want there to be NOTHING to find (although secretly if I don't find anything questionable I suspect she's outsmarted me... just a suspicious mind I guess!)

STRATEGY 4:

Talk About the Elephant in the Room

Our daughters do face real challenges online. We know they are there. They know there are there. We just don't talk about them very much. The more we talk about the elephant in the room the more likely we are to save our daughters from danger. Parents, I promise you that your girls are looking for an adult to delve straight into their world, 'boots and all'.

I have noticed that online problems can go undetected for long periods of time without parents noticing them. I have sat with girls who have been viewing pornography for years without anyone in their lives knowing. I have also sat with girls who have been chronically bullied for months online without anyone knowing. That really makes me sad.

No matter how many contracts we draw up or how much software we install nothing can replace our relationship with our daughters. Our intuition and communication will far outweigh any other strategy we implement. When it comes to social media we have to have eyes in the back of our hearts. And then some. Perception is everything.

One thing we can't stop doing is talking openly about the things that concern us. This won't eliminate the risks but it will reduce the risks. Pornography, sexting, body image, cyberbullying are just some of the issues that have the potential to trip our daughters up. We should never expect our daughters to be the first person to bring up these issues. We have to be the ones who are brave enough to start the conversation. It's your 'check and chat' time.

Choose the time of your conversations carefully but don't procrastinate. The best time might be late at night when the house is quiet or when an older sibling isn't around. The worst time may be when they get home from school or during exam times. However I have noticed how easy it is for mums to let emotions drive them to starting conversations during inappropriate times.

Walking or driving and talking may be easier than talking face-to-face. Some girls are more comfortable in their own bedroom where they are surrounded by familiar things. Personally there are times when I have just put my kids in the car, locked the doors and said, "This is going to take a while so strap in and let's get some food along the way." There was no easy way around some conversations so you just have to jump in and get on with it. There are some talks that have to happen, so be upfront about it. Wade on in. You might just say, "This is going to be an awkward conversation. You can expect it is going to take about half an hour so grab a snack and let's go for a walk." At least it will strike their interest!

Have the mindset that these conversations never really finish. You might say, "If you think about it tomorrow or the next day just bring it up with me again." Whether they take you up on it or not is up to them, but at least you are giving them the choice. A single dad recently told me that his daughter always asks a silly (borderline irrelevant question) before she asks the question she really wants to ask. He said to me, "I know my girl. It's just what she does."

The first time your daughter hears you talk about pornography or sex she is likely to think it's totally weird and awkward, but it is amazing how quickly she will get used to it. Don't be put off by her initial reactions. One shot at a tough topic is never enough so give yourself a few goes at it to get it right. My kids now say, "Here we go (big eye roll)... It is mum's life lessons again." They are so familiar with my off-the-cuff tips on life. The more often we talk about sensitive issues, the more it reminds our daughters that the door is always open to them. It also communicates that we aren't naive to the pressures they are facing.

Mums Write In...

My daughter literally sat on the end of her bed with her back to me the whole time I spoke to her about her periods. She didn't even look at me once. I didn't know whether to stop or keep talking... so I just kept talking. It was so awkward. I thought I had totally failed at the whole thing. It was a big failure moment for me as a mum and I had a tear that night. I decided to never try that again. Two days later to my surprise she came to me and asked me a question about pads. I could have burst into tears!!! I actually think I did have a tear. She was listening. Something I said went in.

STRATEGY 5:

Buy a Radiation Shield

Teenagers who are attached to mobile phones all day every day have some serious health risks. With each phone call more radiation exposure is created. There are enough clinical studies to show increasing evidence that there is a link between mobile phones and certain brain tumours[29].. Because the electromagnetic radiation is invisible the dangers to this exposure are not taken seriously or even thought about. It's the whole, 'out of sight, out of mind' scenario.

Although it is another expense (I can hear you groaning from here) a radiation shield is definitely worth putting on your daughter's phone. Just Google 'radiation shields for phones' and you will find a range of scientifically approved shields to choose from. These shields block harmful radiation, which has to be a good thing for a growing brain!

Mums Write In...

I hadn't thought about this much until I saw a television show where a neurosurgeon was discussing the reasons why he won't use a mobile phone without a headpiece and why he won't allow his children to use one. The brain tumours he operates on every year were certainly enough to put him off and make me think!

STRATEGY 6:

Consider a Toolbox

Mobile phones are DIFFICULT for every family to manage. No sooner do parents feel like they are on top of things than things slip through their fingers again. I want to pause right now to acknowledge how challenged every parent feels. There will be very few families reading this book who don't identify with this pain.

The amount of girls who sleep with their phones in their bedroom and even under their pillow astounds me. It sounds crazy to us adults who crave sleep but our daughters are obsessed with their phones. I challenge you to take your daughter's phone and put it in your room for a night and see how many messages she receives. It may shock you how often it dings at 2am.

These are some of the funny (but not so funny) stories I have recently heard from normal families with normal girls. These girls were not chasing trouble. They just show you how real FOMO (fear of missing out) is. These girls simply didn't want to miss out on one moment of the action:

One of my clients was meant to hand her phone in at 9pm each night. Although she was handing in her phone, she was also taking the SIM card out of it and putting it into another old phone that was in her room. She then proceeded to text her friends throughout the night.

Another mother required her daughter to put her phone on the kitchen bench and turn it off for an hour during homework time. When her daughter would retrieve it and turn it on again there were times when she would receive a backlog of 100 messages. "Thank goodness someone loves me!" she would say.

Another girl would politely put her phone in the laundry at 10pm as asked each night. During the night she would get up and retrieve it so she could text her friends. Her mum found out when she saw some activity online at an unusual hour of the morning.

Our daughters need time away from their phone. They just do. They need to know they can exist without it. They need to be reassured that the world will not fall apart. But how do you get your phone off your daughter? If you put it on the bench she will just get it. Parents have said to me that no matter where they hide their daughter's phone they always find it. So there are times when I have suggested it is in everyone's best interest to buy a toolbox.

The toolbox should be big enough for everyone's technology, not just your daughter's. At dinnertime I would suggest that everyone put their phone in the toolbox and lock it away for an hour. It is far easier to hide a key than a phone.

Parents, our daughters need us to be an example here too. If we want our girls to sleep without a phone and use an alarm clock perhaps we need to use one too. No phone in your room will equal no phone in their room. That goes with phones at the dinner table and spending hours playing games on your phone. If you are an example here you will have more credibility when it comes to pulling them in line.

Mums Write In...

For a number of months I couldn't work out why my daughter didn't want to eat breakfast. I was starting to wonder if she wanted to lose weight. I finally worked it out. She would get up in the morning, have a shower and the first thing she would do was play some snake game on her phone. It's a mindless game but one of those addictive games nonetheless. It took me a while to work out that she would rather keep playing that game than eat breakfast!! After a while she just got used to not eating breakfast and being on the stupid PHONE! That phone is her default when she is bored or has even two minutes spare. It means she has absolutely no down time when it is in her hands. Our daughter's final report card last year was okay, but not as good as it could have been or should have been. We've explained to her that we are sacrificing a lot so she can go to a good (private) school, which we are happy to do, but her part of the bargain is 100% effort, 100% of the time (she will never again brag to me about how she WALKED the entire school cross country despite being quite a capable runner!). The school marks were okay but some of the comments about being disorganised, poorly prepared and homework not done were disappointing and out of character for her. We attributed much of this to the disruption caused by the constant 'bing-bong' during her homework. This year we're taking a much stronger approach. Our daughter will get home from school between 4:30 and 5:00pm and she can keep her phone, iPod connection going until 5:30pm and then she hands over the lot until 8:00pm. She can have them until 9:00pm when they get put into our bedroom until morning. I've told her that if she wants more time she can have them back when she's sitting in the car ready for school the next morning and not before (she can hardly get out of bed as it is to be ready to go on time so I doubt she will be motivated enough to sacrifice sleep at THAT end of the night to LIKE someone else's crap online). Somewhere in amongst managing all this social activity (actual and virtual) we can't lose sight of the REAL stuff they NEED to do. These days I know enough to add the 'I reserve the right to change the rule' disclaimer to EVERYTHING I implement!

STRATEGY 7:

Create a Sexting Safety Plan

Let me give sexting some context. 49% of young people have sent a sexually suggestive image and 67% of young people have received a sexually suggestive image[30].

I want you to take away two things from this statistic. Sexting is a serious issue but a very common one. If your daughter has sent a nude image remember she is not the only one who has done so. Remember too that teenagers can recover from doing so. It is not a mistake that they can't bounce back from. I actually think it can teach them a huge amount of resilience and self-protection if dealt with properly.

While many teenagers say that sending a nude image was exciting and thrilling there is no such thing as safe sexting. The consequences of this type of sexual experimentation can't be ignored and there is definitely a gender bias when it comes to the consequences associated with this issue. I often see girls' reputations damaged in a split second while guys walk away relatively unscathed. I see girls humiliated, violated and at times even blackmailed with nudes. The digital footprint that potential employees can now uncover (for relatively little dollars) is absolutely scary so yes, it is very concerning.

This is a conversation I recently had with a girl after she was caught sexting.

Me: Don't you think it would be better if you spoke to your mum before this gets out.

Teen Girl: But she will kill me.

Me: Yes, she will. (We both laugh)

Me: But after she kills you she will love you lots. In fact the more she kills you the more she will want to love you afterward. It's the way it works with parents. If you can be really brave and get through the killing bit you will get to the loving bit.

Teen Girl: (Smiles) It's true. She always ends up buying me something after I'm in big trouble.

Me: Okay, big breath. Brave girl. Call her.

Parents, this is what I want you to do if you think your daughter might be sexting. Simply ask a very direct question (without a lot of warning or lead in time). "Have you ever sent or received a naked picture?" A direct question gives a teenager zero wiggle room. It also gives parents the best indication as to whether their daughter is lying.

Firstly, reinforce your love for your daughter. All girls appreciate a soft and kind voice, even when a parent has to communicate their disappointment. Girls are expecting the worst and often anticipating harsh anger. My Soft and Close Strategy (Chapter 1: Disrespect - Strategy 2) goes a long way right now.

Once you know what you are dealing with you can respond thoughtfully. I suggest parents handle sexting using my

Seesaw approach (Chapter 1: Disrespect – Strategy 3). You need to assess the positives and keep them intact while reducing the negatives in your daughter's life. You only discipline to ensure the scale is tipping in her favour, not to unleash your wrath or disappointment. In practical terms that might mean introducing some more positives and it might also mean saying a few more 'no's'.

Positive, scheduled daily routine stabilises stressful situations. That means keep everything as normal as possible. Unless there are safety issues to consider don't limit her access to her friends or her usual positive activities. If you can increase the positive activities and keep her busy with safe, fun activities then do it! Also stick to normal wake and bedtimes.

Make sure she is safe. Reinforce your need and desire to protect your daughter by saying no or making any changes you need to ensure her safety. One example that comes to mind is if sexting has happened in a teenager's bedroom at night, perhaps social media needs to have a shut down time and remain out of her bedroom.

The Roller Coast of Emotions

Most parents will feel a sense of shame or anger when they find out their daughter has sent a nude. I have seen parents absolutely torn apart when they found out that their 12 year-old sent a nude to a 15 year-old boy. It is a normal, protective and healthy reaction. However when a parent transfers this emotion to a teenager it doesn't help. Process your emotions away from your daughter so you can be as positive as possible when you are with them.

Lots of constructive talking to a young person goes a long way. This will help them reflect, evaluate and learn from the experience. Sometimes girls show a range of strong emotions including anger, shame, grief and loss and are feeling the weight of their poor choices. Other times they aren't taking things as seriously as their parents are. I have heard a lot of girls say, "It's no big deal", to which I sometimes wonder if things just haven't caught up with them yet.

The Difficult Questions

These are some of the tougher questions that parents ask me, which I am going to try and answer as honestly as I can with the help of great resources like www.esafety.gov.au, which I recommend parents refer to.

Can teenagers or parents recover nude photos?

When it comes to recovering nudes you can do your best but there is no guarantee that you (or the school or even the police) can retrieve or delete them. Schools and police may carry a bit more weight when it comes to retrieving photos but even then there are no guarantees. It depends where they have gone once they have been sent.

What are the legal issues relating to sexting?

It is illegal to ask for, take or create, receive and keep, be in possession of, send or upload a sexually explicit image or video of anyone under the age of 18, even if they are your boyfriend or girlfriend and even if they approve of you doing so. Images include young people showing their private parts, posing in a sexual way, doing a sexual act or being in the presence of someone who is doing a sexual act.

When teenagers sext it is a criminal offense because it creates child pornography. We have to see sexting in this light and treat it seriously. The penalties can include jail sentences and sex offender registration. The police may choose to charge youth with a less serious crime, send them to youth counselling, give them a warning or caution or let their parents or school decide on the consequences. Police are more likely to press serious charges when the incident involves harassment or threats.

When should parents contact the police?

Definitely contact them if your daughter is in any danger, being bullied or threatened or if an image has been spread without her consent. Many parents go to the police in the hope they will be able to retrieve photos, which in some cases police will assist with and other times they are unable to. Authorities see thousands of cases of teenage sexting and are most concerned about young people's safety. They do become very active when bullying or blackmail is involved with sexting.

When should parents contact the school?

Schools have to report incidents of sexting to the police and they will have their own internal policy on associated punishment like expulsion or suspension. It may only be necessary to disclose an incident of sexting if it is likely to become public, impact their education or you needed the school's help to retrieve photos.

When should parents contact other families?

I personally would be very cautious about contacting other families but this is my personal opinion. I also need to say that every situation is different, but I imagine your daughter needs you on her team right now. Refer to my thoughts on this later in this book (Chapter 5: Drugs and Alcohol - Strategy 6). If there is a need to contact another family my guess is that the incident would be serious enough for the school or police to be involved and therefore you could leave that job to them.

What should teenagers do if your daughter receives a nude?

Delete the image or video immediately and let the sender know that they don't wish to receive any more of them. They can also report it to the service that they were posted on. I also recommend they discuss the incident with an adult, but we all know this does not always happen. They should never forward it to someone else.

Prevention

Parents of pre-teens often ask me what they can do to prevent their daughters from sending or receiving nude images. This is a great question! These are just some small tips that will make the most impact:

- Don't be paranoid about sexting
- Create Crystal Clear Agreements (Chapter 2: Social Media - Strategy 2)
- Insist on Transparency (Chapter 2: Social Media - Strategy 3)
- Remember these key things:
    - Negotiate a shut down time
    - Choose a safe place to charge their phone at night
    - Ensure there are no phones in bedrooms (especially at night).
    - Don't be naive. Allow for the possibility that your child could send a nude.

    - Talk to them about nudes and sexting regularly.
    - Be aware of the company they keep and their values.
    - Teach them the difference between beautiful and sexy.
- Be aware of warning signs and high-risk behaviours:
    - Quickly minimised computer screen.
    - Taking a phone to bedrooms and bathrooms.
    - Changing passwords or cracking safety software.
    - Not allowing a phone to leave their side.
    - Showing fear if a parent picks up their phone.

Have eyes in the back of your head and then some.

Mums Write In...

My daughter has an iPod touch. She is 16 years-old and in Year 11 at a private school. We are both working professionals and we consider ourselves to be committed parents. My daughter has her phone with her at school because she needs to call us if she is in trouble on the way home. She leaves it on the bench each night at 9pm. She had a game attached to it called 'Tap It'. I didn't realise it but there was a chatroom attached to the game. I had no idea that chatrooms were attached to games! I often check her phone at the end of the day just to supervise her use of it. I stumbled upon this chatroom and the seedy conversations that were going on! I was horrified. I read what she had just written only moments before... "What are you doing right now? I'm on my bed relieving myself from tension..." I followed her conversation and I realised the amount of information that he had managed to extract from her. She had sent four nudes over the course of two weeks talking to this man. He knew how old she was, what location she lived, what school she went to... Scary, scary stuff for me.

STRATEGY 8:

Promote the Benefits

Technology isn't good or bad. It just is. The values we instil in our children will determine what they do with technology over the next fifty years. Admittedly technology is a huge responsibility and one that our children will have to learn how to handle progressively throughout their life.

Technology will take us wherever our children determine it to go and we do have a great deal of input into that. We have a great part to play in shaping the values that will guide the discovery and future use of technology. If they are going to spend copious amounts of time online (and let's face it, they are) I would rather them be spending it creating an awesome digital footprint that they can be proud of in the future. If your daughter's digital footprint is a real thing then why not encourage her to use it to her advantage?

Just remember it's not all bad and we need not fear it. We hear so much about the downside of being online that we forget that there are also some great benefits. That's why I've started to talk to teenagers about creating an online profile that they can be proud of and will make future employees stand up and take notice. The Internet is no respecter of age, social status or gender, so some of the limits teenagers have in the real world are removed. They can present their ideas and talents to the world right now in a way that truly can make a difference.

If they are budding photographers, why not start an online account or better still sell their work to a photography site? If they are social activists they might like to choose a ghost name and create a blog or podcast to tell their story. Entrepreneurs (and social entrepreneurs) can open online shops, trade second hand wares, fundraise, investigate drop shipping or stocks... and that has to be a far better use of time than playing games or social media.

Mums Write In...

My daughter has a big heart and gets very involved in 'causes'. She is always drawing attention to charities. I am proud to see her do something positive with her time online.

My eldest has started two online businesses. Both came out of something she loves to do. One is still in operation today even though she is now a young adult.

Years ago when my daughter was 13 she started a group chat asking if anyone had been bullied and how it affected them and how they coped. I was so proud.

My daughter has a successful Instagram account for her photography.

My eldest started a local Facebook page for lost and found pets. It has quite a following and it's so heart-warming to see people helping one another by sharing the posts. They have had a lot of success helping owners find their fur-babies.

There was a girl who created an online formal wear site in high school who is now doing really well for herself. She was on Shark Tank.

My daughter decided to create a bonus Instagram account after her friends continued to comment on her ability to give advice and lift their spirits. On their page, people asked advice and she would find uplifting quotes, memes, songs and poems to post. It was quite therapeutic for her for such a long time.

I had a friend whose daughter created a closed group for girls. The concept was for that girl to post a photo and other members commented positively on that photo to boost all the girls' self esteem.

One of my daughter's youth leaders has created a blog to inspire, refresh and motivate young girls to live a greater life. This resource is impacting thousands of girls around the globe each year.

My daughter watches a girl who has her own YouTube channel. It's actually pretty good! It's all about positive self-image and beauty products.

CHAPTER THREE

Sexuality

A Snap Shot of Reality

69% of teenagers have experienced some form of sexual activity[31].

Approximately 25% of Year 10s and 50% of Year 12s have had sexual intercourse[32].

23% of sexually active young people have sex with multiple sexual partners each year[33]. This figure has significantly increased since 2002.

The majority of sexual encounters are happening in homes[34].

Approximately 17% of sexually active teenagers are either drunk or high when they have sex[35].

Approximately one quarter of teenagers between Year 10 and 12 report having unwanted sex[36].

One in two sexually active young people will contract an STI before the age of 25[37].

Approximately 63% of teenagers used a condom the last time they had a sexual encounter[38].

Pornography is now commonplace with research telling us that 84% of boys and 60% of girls accidentally see pornography by the time they are 17 years old[39].

Messages About Sex

It was a Monday. A mother called our office hoping to speak to me about her daughter. My secretary transferred the call to me. Through a steam of tears and apologies for those tears, she told me that her very innocent looking 13 year-old daughter had just had sex with an 18 year-old young man. She couldn't believe this was happening in her family. After all she had sent her daughter to a private school and given her everything she needed to become a mature and responsible woman. I couldn't console her on the phone so I offered to visit her home and see if I could be of some help.

When I arrived at the house mum met me with a box of tissues in her hand. She was really, really sad. She then introduced me to dad. He wasn't sad. He was really, really mad. He was so mad that he had just gone and bought a freshly sharpened axe. True story! It was standing proudly in the garage and he said to me, "Michelle, if your conventional methods don't work I am going to take matters into my own hands!" I believed him.

We decided that it would be my job to tell their 13 year-old Dani that she couldn't keep seeing (and having sex with) an 18 year-old boy. I was expecting a massive tantrum followed by tears. I call it the Romeo and Juliet speech that I've heard so many times before. "He's the love of my life. He completes me. My life will never be the same without him". But her reaction was one I could have never anticipated. Dani simply folded her arms and sighed, "Well if I can't have a boyfriend can I have a mouse?"

My heart skipped a beat. For a minute I forgot to breathe. Did she really say what I thought she had just said? I looked over at her mother to help me comprehend her daughter's words. *What species of child have you produced here?* I thought.

"She has always wanted a pet mouse," mum informed me.

"A pet mouse it is," I responded (although still trying to make the connection).

Please don't tell me that a mouse was going to be the answer to this illegal situation. Please, please don't tell me that I could swap an eighteen year-old boyfriend with a pet mouse and everyone was going to be happy!! To me that just didn't make sense.

But the more I talked with Dani the more I realised she saw sex very differently than I did. Dani saw sex as entertainment, something that added interest to her life. A pet mouse could do that, couldn't it? She thought she could trade and negotiate with sex in order to get more of what she wanted. Sex was a commodity. Nothing more and nothing less! I could only conclude that she had become overexposed and desensitised to sex's value.

If I were to open the mind of the average teenager and dissect their understanding of sex I think most parents would get a shock. Parents fall into the trap of thinking that this generation 'sees' sex the same way they did. Parents also fall into the trap of thinking their teenager 'sees' sex the way they want them to 'see' sex or have advised them to see sex. Sorry parents – not so. This generation has done a complete 360 on how they see gender and sexuality. It's one of the biggest changes in their culture.

If you really want to know how your teenager 'sees' sex it will only take you a few minutes. Google it. Go on... just punch it in. Make a few clicks and see what comes up. Then go and watch some of the movies, television shows, and music video clips they watch and listen to the lyrics of the songs they sing. This is the information that influences your teenager's perception of sex. Truly you say? That can't be so. There is no way my daughter could know that stuff. I haven't brought her up that way.

I know you think you are the only one bringing up your daughter but unfortunately there is another influence in her life. It lives in her pocket (all day long). There are some really clear messages that the online world is giving our daughters about sex and relationships. We have to clearly understand these messages and be prepared to engage in conversations about them.

Message 1 - Sex is a Purely Physical Experience

There is a great pressure on our daughters to perceive sex as a purely physical experience – full stop. There is a great deal of pressure to 'put out' without any expectation of commitment or a relationship in return. I see many girls force themselves to perform to this expectation. When teenagers buy into the concept that sex is simply a physical experience it opens the door to reckless experimentation. That means that one-night stands and hook ups are not just for a few game ones. It is expected as a normal part of growing up. Oral sex or anal sex is seen as entry level.

Message 2 - Sexual Experience is Attractive

There is also a great deal of pressure for girls to be sexually experienced and have knowledge about sex. Young people who don't have this knowledge are often teased and ridiculed leaving them more vulnerable to using the internet as a source of sexual information, in turn becoming more vulnerable to pornography addictions. I have sat with many girls in my office who have become addicted to pornography after using the online world as an education tool because their innocence wasn't popular.

In previous generations, boys were more likely to be the ones who parents needed to pull into line and talk to about their relentless pursuit of the opposite sex. Today our girls are also doing the pursuing. They feel the pressure to initiate sex and pursue boys rather than be called a 'prude' or 'frigid'. Girls are pushing these boundaries of their sexuality and they feel 'out of it' or like they are missing out if they don't want to get involved.

There is an entirely new sexually active young lady who is emerging. They are using the boys just as much as the boys are using them. They wear their sexual experiences like a badge of honour. It's not uncommon for girls to announce they are going to have sex and then choose the boy they want to have it with and hunt them down. I have seen girls send nudes to boys and then tell teachers they were being harassed to send them, which has ended up with the boys being suspended until the truth eventually came out.

Message 3 - Sex Is Not Always Private

To me one of the biggest changes between past generations and this generation is how public people's sexual lives have become. What was once thought of a private experience is now accepted as public. It is okay to have sex on camera in front of the whole world. In fact you get an academy award for it. It is okay to talk about your sexual experiences online. You can actually build a huge following by doing it and earn a lot of money.

Our daughters so easily get involved in sexual activity online without giving it a second thought. The reason is that they don't see sex as something that is private; they see it is something that is okay for it to be shared on a public forum. Parents often are very shocked to find out their teenagers are involved in any type of dirty talk or activity online simply because it is not what they would have done at their age.

When you follow the messages of teenagers you can see how things get messy. Teenagers share intimate information on their social pages at lightning speed, without giving it a second thought. They expose themselves to their friends in a way they would never do in a face-to face-conversation. It's almost like they believe the words that they write don't carry any concrete weight in the real world.

It often baffles me as to why parents are shocked to hear their daughters are involved in sexting. They see naked photos of other people so often so why not send their own? They are simply desensitised to the gravity and impact of sexual activity and nudity. They don't realise that with the push of a button everyone's life can change until it's too late. It is just too easy for them not to get involved.

Message 4 – Sexy is Beautiful

If my boyfriend asked me for a photo of myself when I was 14, it would have been one with clothes on. Never would it have crossed my mind to give him nude images. Times have definitely changed.There has emerged confusion between the words beautiful and sexy. In fact sexy is the new beautiful. More and more of our girls are wanting to be perceived as 'hot', 'attractive' and 'grown up'.

Photos have now become the big thing in our girls' lives. No longer do our girls get given a school photo of themselves once a year to scrutinize. Now days, social media demands a constant stream of photos and the sexier the photos the more friends they tend to attract. Everyone wants to be friends with the girl who has eyes that pop and lips that pout.

One father dropped his son off to a party and watched the 15 year-old girls arrive looking like hookers. He was speaking to another father who was also dropping his son off. They jokingly said, "Gosh, I wish girls looked like this when I was 15. What's going on here?" Sexy is seen as beautiful. Our girls have blurred those concepts together. They don't see a distinction between the two and I am seeing younger and younger girls try the sexy look in order to be beautiful.

But let me say that the confusion between sexy and beautiful doesn't just impact girls. Boys are under just as much pressure to buff up, get a six-pack and be sexy. It's a pressure that undermines their confidence as they don't feel like they can measure up to the girls in their grade who look years older than they do.

It is a huge challenge to keep a teenager's concept of beauty realistic, balanced and undistorted. Magazines, video clips and advertising all bombard our girls with images of Photo-shopped perfection, which our girls compare themselves to.

That is why there is not a week that doesn't go by where a mum doesn't talk to me about her frustrations about shopping for clothes with her daughter. Girls are surrounded by images of distorted sexualised beauty. The truth is, sexy is not beautiful on a 13 year-old. It's just downright inappropriate.

The New Sex Educator

The introduction of the smart phone has definitely changed the way our girls discover and explore their sexuality. While speaking to a group of Year 8 girls who were in the thick of their peer pressure years I asked them to come up with a list of ten big decisions they had to make about sex. Their responses were heavily linked to their Internet activity.

Here is a list of the ten big decisions they identified...

Decision 1: Whether to talk to someone they don't know online about sex.
Decision 2: Whether to post a sexy photo online.
Decision 3: Whether to flirt on text message.
Decision 4: Whether to send back a naked photo of yourself when someone asks for it.
Decision 5: Whether to keep passing on a pornographic image, which is sent to you.
Decision 6: Whether to participate in phone sex with a stranger or boyfriend.
Decision 7: Whether to meet with someone I don't know after flirting online.
Decision 8: Whether to let the boys on the school bus touch me on the way home.
Decision 9: Whether to hook up at late night (shopping centre on Thursday night).
Decision 10: Whether to kiss another girl just to try it.

The Internet has become a major sex educator of our kids. The answers to all their questions are only a click of a button away. Unfortunately, the type of sexual content our daughters have been exposed to online is far broader than the traditional birds and bees information. Sex isn't only depicted as sexual intercourse between two people in a loving relationship. It has expanded into a variety of sexual experiences including friends with benefits, hook ups, faux lesbianism, bestiality, sexting and phone sex. Most of which is quite foreign to parents who enjoy the good old-fashioned version!

The accessibility of pornography is a real issue for this generation. Please don't ignore it parents. Sometimes our own stereotypes limit our ability to see this generation's needs. Mothers look at me shocked when I tell them it is no longer a gender specific issue. "You're right," they have replied thoughtfully. "I have had this talk with my son but I have never thought to have this conversation with my daughter, but she has access to exactly the same material. Do girls really look at this stuff these days?" Sad to say I am seeing more and more girls in their early 20s addicted to pornography, stemming from decisions they made in their early teen years when they have been feeling either sad, lonely, rebellious or inquisitive.

Many of today's girls have access to pornography via their phones 24/7. Even if they choose not to access it they often still get sent pornography from friends or strangers. They used to have to seek it out - now it seeks them out. Very few escape exposure. Pornography is now commonplace with research telling us that 100% of young people see pornography by the time they are 16 years-old. Unfortunately it has become a very normal part of young people's introduction to sex.

We have to once again stop and realise the difference between pornography we may have seen as a teenager and the pornography our young people are viewing. Pornography in today's world is on the whole much more explicit, with live videos rather than still images easily attainable. It leaves less to the imagination and it is far easier to get your hands on 'creepy' porn that is violent and degrading. This is far different than stealing a *Playboy* magazine because you wanted to know what boobs looked like.

Pornography is impacting our teenagers' view of sex and in many cases directly impacts sexual experimentation[40]. It is impossible for young people to view pornography and not have it affect how they view the opposite sex. Impossible! It doesn't just impact one area of their lives or stay neatly tucked away in secret. It impacts everything and every area in their life. I always tell young people that what they watch in private is the most obvious thing about them.

This is honestly with not one bit of docketing, the list of questions I received from private school students last year. I was asked to answer these questions during a sexual health conference for Year 10 students. These were questions that the students anonymously asked and the school had chosen to address. It makes you wonder which ones they had left out?

Q. How do you tell your parents that you're sexually active?
Q. How do you tell them that you think you could be pregnant?
Q. How do you tell your parents that you think you could have a disease?
Q. Is it weird to have feelings for my cousin?
Q. Why is it wrong to have feelings for someone who is out of the legal age limit?
Q. Can you contract diseases from the same sex?
Q. If I swallow sperm what happens?
Q. What's bad about anal?
Q. Are threesomes so bad?

Q. Is it possible to have intercourse with an animal?
Q. I have sexual feelings for my dog of three years. I have dreams about doing doggie style.
Q. How do I orgasm faster?
Q. Is watching porn good? I watch it with friends and I can't see what's wrong with it.
Q. Is masturbating okay? I enjoy it and do it most nights.
Q. Do you get in trouble for sexting? How much trouble?
Q. Is it normal to have gay dreams about my friends?

When I read questions like this it makes me think about where our daughters' head space is at, what they perceive as normal and how we can best support them through the decisions that they make everyday. I want our girls to have a healthy respect for who they are and value themselves as precious, special and valuable. I would hate to think that they would think less of themselves than they ought.

Fantasy and Reality

The media has influenced our children like no one else could have ever influenced them. Our kids are marking the first generation in history to have been exposed to sexual content through online media and researchers are already noting that exposure to pornography sustains young people's adherence to unhealthy ideas of sex and relationships[41].

What concerns me is that our daughters have, in many ways, already lost their innocence before they hit 13 because of the content they are exposed to online. When conducting sexual health classes for primary aged students I am often shocked at the depth of knowledge that Year 6 students have. The movies and television shows they are watching are leaving young minds with questions about relationships and sex that they often answer amongst themselves. I find that by the time most children are 10 years-old they are well and truly educating each other through their everyday discussions.

One of the problems with consistently exposing children to sexual material is that they become desensitised to the value of sex. When we desensitise our children to sex it creates a range of problems. One of the biggest problems is that our children go from revering sex to being very casual about it. They become so casual that they no longer see or fear the real risks and they no longer value it or appreciate its beauty. Sex loses its novelty and awe... it becomes common. In the words of a teenager, "Sex is no big deal mum. Everyone is doing it."

A mother I recently met summed it up perfectly when she asked me, "What's changed with our girls? We were scared to have sex. We were scared to get pregnant. We didn't want to be 'that girl' who was called 'loose' or a 'whore'. Having your first kiss was a big deal and this generation seems to think giving your first blowjob is no big deal. They just don't regard sex as sacred at all! The fear factor is definitely gone and they seem to be living, breathing and talking about sex on the Internet."

Today's teenagers have developed very different beliefs about sex to the generations before them. Although these beliefs may have been discovered and fostered through the media they aren't just staying in fantasy-land. Teenagers literally try to live the dream and transfer these beliefs into their everyday lives. They allow these beliefs to guide the choices they make especially if they don't have an adult support person who has a strong influence in their lives.

Many of the teenagers I meet think they are going to have sex and wake up the next day and life is going to be better. Just like the movies. In reality it doesn't always play out like this and it pains me to be with a girl the next day who says, "Why didn't someone tell me! I'm sore. I'm scared. I'm not sure if we are going to stay together. I'm not sure what he is going to say about me. I wish I hadn't done that!" Or a boy who says, "What now? I don't even know if I like her and she won't stop texting me. This feels really confusing."

The truth is that someone probably did tell them that sex was complicated but more people told them that is was fun. More people told them that sex was a great experience. More people told them that they wouldn't feel any different in the morning. That means that more people didn't talk about the consequences of the break up, the rumours and the regret. More people didn't tell them that a one-second-slip-up, that 'going with the flow', that an irreversible decision can impact the rest of their life.

We need to make sure we keep talking to our daughters about the real-life consequences of all their decisions, including sex. Life and relationships don't always turn out ideally. That is why we need to make sure we ask them the hard questions and talk about things like unplanned pregnancy, sexually transmitted infections and broken hearts. It is only after the event that many girls recognise that the film clip they just saw and the experience they just had is vastly different. Let's face it, none of their celebrity icons have sexually transmitted infections. That's why talking, educating and combating the media driven, money-making attitudes and ideas our kids are sold is so, so important.

We all want our girls to grow into confident young women. I believe this starts with the cleanest slate possible. Protecting them from unhealthy, damaging or foolish sexual choices before they hit sexual maturity is a critical part of every parent's job. Helping them gain a respect for themselves is imperative to each person's journey.

STRATEGY 1:

Keep a Poker Face

"What's wrong with having sex?" 13 year-old Emma blurts out.

Mum's eyebrows rise as she thinks, "Should I really answer that, now, in the shopping centre?"

Keep a poker face. Play it cool. Maybe I heard her wrong.

Maybe she said, "What's wrong with cousin Rex?" Nah... we don't have a cousin Rex. I definitely heard, "What's wrong with having sex?" I hope she doesn't mean what's wrong with having sex this weekend?

As adults, we know that sex at the right time, right place and with the right person is a beautiful thing. Yet sex at the wrong time, wrong place with the wrong person can be very damaging. Our girls are often questioning whether that piece of advice is in fact true.

Sexual exploration usually starts internally not externally. As our girls grow into young women they begin questioning the beliefs and values we handed to them as children. They are, heaven forbid, developing their own moral compass. Most parents hope their daughters will adopt the beliefs they were brought up with in a peaceful and agreeable manner. As we know from personal experience part of growing up means discovering the world for ourselves.

It is not unusual for 13 year-old girls to be asking themselves deep questions like: how do I feel about one night stands? Living together? Marriage? Would I ever have an affair? What are my views on rape and paedophilia? If you listen carefully you will hear their internal dialogue spill out in the most peculiar times and places. Their incidental questions and comments are often indications of greater internal soul searching going on behind the scenes.

When our daughters ask, "What's so bad about having sex?" they are often genuinely asking, "What experiences haven't I had that make me unable to see the risks?" They genuinely want the gaps in their experiences to be filled in with conversation and discussion. What they need from us as parents is patience and honesty, especially during times when their opinions differ from ours.

One issue we need to get more comfortable talking about is homosexuality and transgender issues. Openness and acceptance of homosexuality and transgender issues mark a very significant shift in today's society. This openness has really defined this generation in so many ways. Our daughters are now learning about these issues in school, which would be unheard of in previous generations. They are thinking through their sexual feelings at ages where all I can remember doing at that age was playing hop scotch.

Early sex education has led to greater empathy towards others who may be bullied for their sexual differences. It has enabled expression and clarification for those who may be searching for answers. It has also given our girls more information to process at younger and younger ages. When I was young I would have never considered the options of pansexual, demisexual, monosexual, bisexual, asexual, autosexual or graya sexual! Young people want (and need) to talk about sexual differences, options and how this impacts their lives.

I had a girl in my office this week whose close friend had just identified as bi-sexual at 15-years-old. She had told her, my client, that she liked another girl in their grade and that she wanted to start a sexual relationship with her. My client was a bit taken back by the whole thing. She really needed someone to talk to about how this might affect the dynamics of their friendship circle and their reputation as a group. She wasn't sure how her friend's mum was going to react either. The worst thing was that she didn't know how to talk to her mum about it. She really wanted to talk to her mum but she didn't know how to approach the subject.

Parents who have brought their children up with religious beliefs or a strict code of values may struggle most with open discussion about sexuality. They will want to tell their daughters that there is one way to think and behave. Full stop. They clearly look at society and determine this is not true. Where that may seem a great way to protect them it isn't a great way to ensure you stay connected to them. Teenagers will be more likely to talk to parents who are open minded, calm, empathetic and up for a discussion about differences.

Our daughters need to have conversations about values, homosexuality, transgender issues, respect, consent, rape and assault in a relaxed, non-judgemental context. Research clearly tells us that the more we talk to our children about sex the more likely they are to wait and the less likely they are to make an impulsive decision under pressure[42].

When having conversations parents need to remember this generation has a lot of empathy. They get very intense about equality and may debate with a level of compassion that many adults don't have. Also remember that just because they talk about it, it doesn't mean they are going out tomorrow to do it. Play it cool mums and dads and keep them talking and processing with you rather than with their friends. The choices they make with regard to their sexuality will shape the rest of their lives.

Mums Write In...

My daughter's friend identifies as bisexual. She likes a girl in her grade but I don't think it's a good thing. I'm personally very uncomfortable watching it. The girl is almost hunting her down like prey. If it were a boy approaching her like that I would be very protective of her. I think that saying no to the same sex, when the fall out amongst your friends could be significant, puts this strategy into a whole new light. Same sex relationships and the dynamics between girlfriends at school is something we didn't deal with very often when we were young. I am watching girls navigate this now and it really concerns me how much more savvy they have to be. I guess that is what you are saying Michelle, we have to be talking to them more.

STRATEGY 2:

Tell Her She is Beautiful

Should you or should you not call your daughters pretty? This was the question I was asked by a wonderful radio announcer a few years ago. He was determined to get to the bottom of the matter, which was a hot topic at the time. The topic got my attention because I had two nieces who at the time were little, cute and incredibly pretty. The very thought of not being able to call them pretty was unthinkable. I watched family members goo and ga over them on a weekly basis!

My answer was this. Please don't stop calling them pretty. A woman's beauty is an incredibly powerful and important asset. In saying that, don't let it be the first or only compliment you give her. Don't let her put all her eggs in the one pretty basket! There are a lot of other qualities girls need to discover in order to reach their potential in life. A woman's appearance is only one of her attributes.

Teaching a girl that it is the first thing that you notice about her gives her the message that her looks are the most important quality that she has. It also reinforces the pretty and perfect stereotype is necessary to live up to.

I think it is interesting to compare the compliments we give boys and girls. Do we encourage our girls to be strong, courageous, brave, daring or smart? Do we encourage our girls to take risks? I have watched boys concuss themselves on the rugby field and then continue to play sport. I also watch their fathers cheer on this commitment to sport and manhood. (much to my horror at times!) I wonder if they would encourage their daughters in the same way? I highly doubt it.

We want to make sure our girls don't take the back seat to their own detriment or rely on their looks instead of their other great attributes. Encourage girls to be all that they are, which is beautiful as well and all those other things that make them a unique and valuable human being.

Mums Write In...

I think we have to be careful about how we approach our daughters' beauty. We know that beauty is in the eye of the beholder and mums and dads are always going to think that their daughters are beautiful, which is absolutely fine. What I really don't like to see is when mums (and it's usually mums) call their daughters 'princess'. THEY ARE NOT ROYALTY! These girls are being raised to think that they are a princess and this comes with all the rights of royalty. I know that this may seem a little far-fetched but girls do believe that they have some sort of royal rights and I bet these same mums aren't calling their sons 'princes!' Bring them down to earth and call them by their names or a cute nick name if you have to but please steer away from calling them a princess!!!!

STRATEGY 3:

Establish Go To Outfits

Many, many parents fight on a regular basis about their daughters' fashion choices. Parents tell me that their girls' shorts are getting shorter and their tops are getting lower. I hear about girls being sent back into their rooms to get dressed again and again. They think they look beautiful. Their parents think they look sexy. I have to remind parents that sexy is the new beautiful. They aren't trying to be inappropriate. They are just copying what they see online.

How your daughter profiles herself does matter, so it is worth helping her develop good dress sense. My shopping rule is this: if I can see up it, down it or through it I'm not buying it. By default these three regulations give you a lot of opportunity to teach your daughter how to dress.

Clothes shopping with a teenage girl can give mothers a headache. I personally think hiring a stylist for an hour can be a really good use of money (and emotional energy) but if you are up for the task don't go shopping without a plan and take these tips with you:

- Find their most comfortable style and stick to it.
- Know what you are shopping for before you go shopping.
- Online shopping is a good starting point.
- Buy the basics first. If you are going to invest money invest it into basics.
- Think outfits not single items.Teenagers need to see

complete outfits together.

- Finish off outfits with the right accessories.
- Shop appropriately for the event or occasion.
- Be honest about whether it suits her body shape or not.
- Know what each item is worth. Don't pay too much.
- There is always tomorrow. If in doubt leave it in the store.

One mum told me that she asks her daughter to establish a few go-to outfits every season, which gets her through meltdown days. These go-to outfits are for hormonal times when girls have nothing to wear, even though their bedroom floors are completely covered in beautiful clothes. This way if girls are in an indecisive mood (which comes around at least every month) they can then pull out their go to outfit and know that they picked it while being in the right frame of mind.

Mums Write In...

With two girls in our family of varying ages it has always been a challenge to come to some sort of agreement in what they are going to wear when they leave the house. A lot of the problems come from dad, as he really doesn't seem to get girls fashion and what he does see he certainly doesn't agree with! I know deep down that she will sometimes sneak the banned clothes into the bag or perhaps even borrow her friend's clothes when she arrives at her house but at the end of the day I have always tried to set a standard which means I put my cleavage away. I am hoping they will go through these fashion faux pas stages but if I keep leading by example they will eventually follow.

STRATEGY 4:

Cheer On Sass and Hair Flicks

I sat with a girl a little while ago who had been flirting with a boy a few months prior at a party. During this party he deliberately got her drunk, lured her away into the bushes and had sex with her. She had some recollection of the whole thing and was expecting that the night's adventures meant he was now her boyfriend.

He decided to post his cryptic version of their get together online in quite crass terms, which humiliated her. Soon after he asked her to be his 'friend with benefits' and meet up with him again. Slight jerk! Stories like these make my blood boil and I tend to go into protective mum mode.

Unfortunately too many girls I sit with tolerate this kind of behaviour. They don't seem to see it as abusive. They seem to think it is normal to be treated this way. I can't believe how many teenagers would rather be treated terribly by the opposite sex in order to be accepted. I hear so many girls say to me that they feel okay with guys taking advantage of them. They honestly know it is happening and they are in the moment that it is happening, okay with it. They say to me that they feel it is normal.

A young girl I have been working with shared a story about how she was surrounded by a group of boys who were egging her on and asking her to touch their penises. They were fully clothed and in their eyes it was all a joke. They were like a pack of wolves bullying her, not allowing her outside of their circle until she did. I was amazed to hear that instead of being angry or upset she actually said that she felt that she liked the attention and that touching the boys just felt like the expected and normal thing to do. The boundaries were obviously blurred.

At that moment she didn't feel like she was doing anything too wrong. She just impulsively did what they asked and in a few minutes the whole thing was over, until later. A girl who was watching on called her a slut online and the story got round the whole school. The next day the boys continued to ask her to touch them thinking she was now an easy target. One boy standing beside the tuckshop said, "If you touch me I'll buy you something." Another said, "Come on I know you want some fun." She was being called a whore at every turn. She was humiliated. The next day it didn't feel so okay. She didn't feel okay.

Situations like these where girls obviously get taken advantage of make me so determined to help our girls see their value. It is scary to think that our girls can get taken advantage of just because they are too nice and just want to fit in. I have to remind girls that there are times when manners are NOT appropriate and that the other person's feelings are NOT the priority.

Below is a text message between a young lady and her boyfriend. They had been going out for about eight months when her boyfriend decided he wanted to take things to the 'next level'. She really wasn't ready for that commitment so she declined his offer politely. They talked about it late into the night, over and over and over. She didn't want to lose him or offend him. She just wasn't ready. She thought she might be ready one day but not right now. He didn't take well to it and no matter how nicely she tried to reject him she eventually decided she would have to change tact. The straightforward approach was going to be the only way to go.

I use this illustration as an example of how to say 'no', teenage style, with a bit of SASS and a hair flick. Our daughters need to understand that words like "I don't think so"; "I'll think about it"; and "Maybe" don't mean no. All they communicate to a guy is that a girl is thinking about them! The louder the 'no' the easier it is for a guy to understand and the easier it is for a girl to walk away with her head held up high.

This is the original screen shot of the message, which I took in my office many, many years ago.

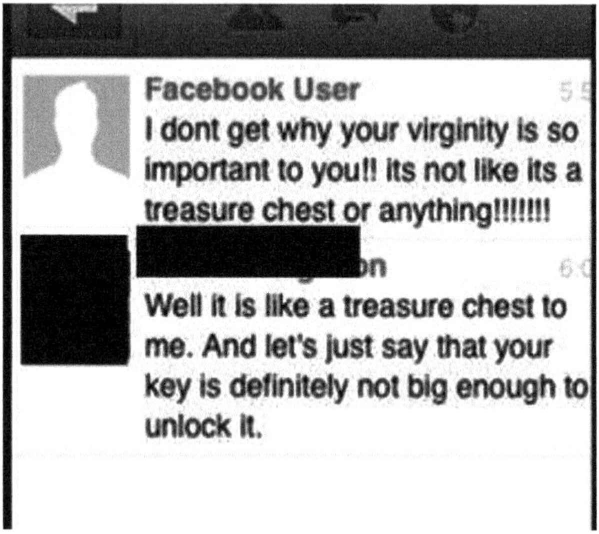

It is horrible to think that our girls could be giving their bodies in exchange for acceptance and that under pressure they are likely to say yes just because they want to be liked rather than because they want to have sex. But the truth is that our girls thrive on acceptance. They could be settling for less because they want to belong and or because they don't know how to say 'no' in a way that makes them feel proud of themselves.

If they say 'no' in exactly the same way that they would say 'no' to their mum if she asked them to clean their room or do their homework, they will do just fine. They just have to use the same amount of sass and attitude. I always tell girls that there are times it is appropriate to be impolite. There are times where it is okay to not be liked. This was one of those times.

Mums Write In...

I'm the happiest dad alive at the moment. My daughter just broke up with her boyfriend. She came to me a few months ago and told me she wanted to go out with this guy. I didn't react. She said she was surprised I didn't react but I said that I raised her well and knew she would pick a nice guy. I did ask when he was going to ask me he could take her out!!! (haha) He did come home and ask!! Over the last few months I noticed that she was struggling. Little things like headaches, irritated and not sleeping well. I could see this boy wasn't good for her. She sees a psychologist and I think she spoke to her about it. She didn't say anything to me. I didn't push it but I just started being around more. I also was just careful where she was and made sure I was always there to pick her up and shake his hand. Today she came to me and said she broke off with him. I couldn't be happier!

STRATEGY 5:

Be Protective

One of my client's daughters had her first boyfriend in Year 8. Her mother thought he was a nice guy. He probably was. They arranged to study together so she dropped her off at his house. His mother was home. All appeared good.

The next day her daughter was dumped on text. When her daughter received the text she broke into tears and ran to the bathroom to tell her friend. Mum listened with horror through the closed bathroom door as she found out that her daughter had had sex with her ex-boyfriend instead of studying!

These are, word for word, her daughter's reflective thoughts after the event. I personally wrote them down with her so I could share them with other girls. My hope was that they offer some insights and help other girls think through what drives their decision-making. They are of course from her perspective and I am sure the guy has a completely different perspective...

- The more attention a boy gives you and the nicer he is to you the harder it is to say *no*.
- It makes me *feel bad* for saying *no*.
- All boys are really, really nice to you at first.
- You like the attention you are getting but you don't like what you have to give to get the attention.
- You say something you don't mean or don't want to say under pressure or in a weak moment.

- Boys will take what you said seriously and keep pursuing and pushing until they get what they want.They persistently wear you down.
- In a weak moment you are likely to say 'yes' when you really mean 'no' because you want the attention to continue.

Please keep sexual experimentation in mind when you allow your daughter to go to a boyfriend's house. I have unfortunately seen some sad things take place when parents have thought their kids were safe and in fact weren't. Young people are at most risk in homes[43]. Could you innocently be putting your daughter at risk while they are working on assignments, going to gatherings or parties that perhaps needed supervision when there was none?

I see so many mums feel romantic (and even proud) when their daughters get a boyfriend in Year 7, 8 and 9 but they don't always take into account that teenage relationships quickly become about sexual experimentation. It isn't long before the pressure to hold hands, kiss and make out becomes a reality. It's our job as parents to carefully consider where are daughters are placed developmentally to handle this pressure.

Our daughters are usually struggling to find their identity and are often driven by a desire to fit in. They haven't clearly defined who they are and what they want out of life so this makes them vulnerable to saying 'yes' to things they aren't sure about. They may feel anxious and unsure about sexual activity but they often push through the warning signs to be accepted. No matter how many times they hear, "If in doubt say no" they may compromise what they really want when they are in a pressured moment. They often feel like they have a point to prove with their peers. There are many times when their peers' opinions matter more than their own.

The limbic system is the most active area of their brain during puberty and dominates decision-making. That means that their emotions are screaming at them the loudest. This, combined with surging hormones, makes teenage relationships hit and miss. We want to keep reinforcing that any sexual activity is a huge decision and should never be made on impulse.

While almost half of teenagers reflect feeling good, happy, fantastic or loved after their last sexual encounter[44], this is not the case for everyone. Of teenagers who have sex before age 16, 38% of girls and 20% of boys say that they regret their first time[45]. When sexually experienced teenagers in the United States were asked whether they wished they had waited longer to lose their virginity, approximately two thirds said 'yes'[46]. Who would have thought?

What if my daughter likes girls? My advice for parents whose daughters are expressing homosexual feelings or who have a same sex partner is this: the same boundaries should apply for heterosexual relationships and gay relationships. That means the same transparency with parents when it comes to their girl's feelings for other girls and the same boundaries when it comes to sleep overs and outings. This often goes amiss because parents aren't used to being this open and even making the same correlations.

Unnecessary damage and hurt can happen with lack of communication, supervision and protection of our kids. A protective parent is a good parent. There is nothing wrong with healthy, sensible boundaries. Even the law recognises that young people under the age of consent need protecting, as they don't yet have the full capacity to make decisions about sexual activity.

Mums Write In...

My eldest daughter told me a few years ago that house parties are so incredibly dangerous. I was shocked. I mean aren't the parents there and supervising? Apparently the parents are always told to stay away and give us our privacy!! "Don't you trust us mum? We are just all sitting around and listening to music!" The dangers with these house parties are threefold. Firstly there is always alcohol – no matter how much you think that there isn't. They sneak it in, in the most ingenious ways. Secondly there are numerous random hook-ups with whoever they feel is providing the most attention, and thirdly it is nothing for sex to happen in the back garden bush / shrubbery and then just get on with the rest of the party!

STRATEGY 6:

Talk About Contraception

Although most parents have braced the subject of sex before their daughters' first serious boyfriend it takes on a whole new meaning when a young man is in their lives. What was a general conversation has now become more relevant. You don't want to fumble your way around this one. Know exactly how you are going to get the conversation started. Realise that you may be met with shoulder shrugs and eye rolls to start with. If this happens just keep talking and be assured that eye rolls don't affect their ability to hear you.

You might like to choose a direct approach, "I can see how quickly you are growing up. I'd like to sit down and talk more openly about sex with you. How about we go out and have a chat?" Or you might like to try a softer approach by asking, "At what age do most young people become sexually active these days? I can imagine it is something that is becoming more common as you get older."

I'm not keen on teenagers having sex in high school because of the emotional, social and physical damage that often comes with it. If you share my view there is nothing wrong with being honest with your daughter. However it is important you let her know that she is ultimately responsible for her decisions. Regardless of her choices reassure her that you will always be there for her.

If there is any chance she is going to have sex make sure you give her full accurate information about contraception and safe sex measures to reduce the risk of STIs and pregnancy. It is so important that your daughter knows you aren't naive and that she can come to you anytime she needs to in order to take care of her body. Do some research and be armed with facts rather than just emotion before you talk to her.

You may want to suggest she visit a doctor to get additional information about contraception, pap smears and STIs. A big part of any doctor's visit is to administer and explain the possible side effects of contraception.

However a visit to a doctor's surgery with your daughter can be a really emotional experience for a parent, especially if you are not happy with your daughter's decision to have sex. Preparing yourself for the reality of the visit is essential. Your daughter is no longer the little girl who held your hand or sat on your lap during a doctor consultation. Doctor's visits involve legalities of age and confidentiality, so you may be asked to leave the room while the doctor privately discusses contraception. This can be really hard for parents especially when they pay for the visit!

Remember that your daughter is learning independence. She is also learning to speak for herself and interact with a medical professional herself. If you do stay in the room doctors may direct questions to your daughter instead of you. They may also make decisions with your daughter that may override your preferences. These can be really hard things for parents to experience.

Parents, please be grateful that there is a reliable support person in your daughter's life to offer expert advice about her health and wellness. That is a blessing.You can help create a positive doctor's experience by being prepared mentally for the process ahead. Don't let it be a bone of contention between you and your daughter. If she is old enough to have sex, she has to be old enough to look after her body.

Mums Write In...

My daughter is 15 and has recently fallen for a really lovely boy. Our family all really like him and he's very respectful but two months in I'm wondering if they're sleeping together. He's not allowed to stay over – even in another room - but they go to parties and out for the evening. I want to ensure she's not being pressured into doing something she doesn't want and that she's all clued up about contraception. What do I say? I don't want to put the idea of having sex in her head so I have to tread carefully. If I am wrong what would she think of me even suggesting that?

STRATEGY 7:

Listen to Your Intuition (ALWAYS)

I'd like to start by saying this is a true story but one which may raise your eyebrows a little. I haven't chosen this story to scare you as a parent. I have chosen it because it illustrates how incredibly valuable the role of perception is when raising a teenager. An intuitive parent is absolutely irreplaceable in a teenager's life. Nothing can do the job that intuition does. Nothing!

Like many 14 year-old girls, Bec was pushing the boundaries and values that she had been brought up with. She hated everyone in her family and rejected anything that resembled common sense. She wanted total freedom and the right to make her own choices. She believed that when it came to her life and her body she had the right to do whatever she liked with it.

Her blatant rebellion was a great concern to her loving family who were working overtime to keep her safe from herself. They were very sensible parents who were alarmed by their daughter's irrational thinking and lack of respect. They knew she would somehow grow out of it but in the meantime had to do their best to love and guide her. There were many days which her family would prefer to forget, none any less than this day...

It was school holidays and Bec told her mum she was going

to the local store. She left through the front door. Her mother didn't give it a second thought. When she arrived home about 20 minutes later she sat on the lounge, texting furiously. Her mother looked at her once and then stopped to take a second look. Something was different about her daughter, but what?

The weirdest, most bizarre thought flashed through her mother's mind. My daughter has just had sex. Then the facts flashed through her mind. She has been gone for 20 minutes it's unlikely she would be that organised! Then the prick of a parent's conscience flashed through her mind. "Why am I thinking like this? My daughter wouldn't do that. Would she?"

But unable to shake the feeling, she decided to check up on her daughter by asking, "Where did you just go?"

"Der...I just went to the corner store..." was her response. "What's it to you?"

"You took a while," her mother questioned. "Did you go anywhere else?"

"Nope."

Call it a hunch. Call it intuition. Her mother was not convinced.

That night Bec's mother shared her concerns about her daughter's sexual activity with her father. "There was something about the way she looked and the way she spoke to me when I questioned her," Bec's mother said. "I can't put my finger on it but she was different when she came home."

The father looked at the facts. "It couldn't be possible," he concluded. "Bec couldn't go to the corner store and come home having had sex! You are being paranoid. She's rebellious but she wouldn't do that!"

It is easy to compile a list of facts about our daughters: where they have been? What they have said? What they have done? That is fairly easily done. However it is much more difficult to see beyond the facts. It is much more difficult to add instinct to facts.

Intuition is often the factor that separates the great parents from the greatest parents. These parents see things that others can't and they are able to respond to these things quickly before others understand what is happening. That is how they stay on top of things and one step ahead.

Being intuitive is not about being paranoid, imagining things or making things up. Intuition is able to capture details that others miss. Intuition captures the things that teenagers don't say, the slight changes in their routine or friendship groups, and the small inconsistencies in their communication or habits. It is about being attentive to the tiniest of changes. Without intuition parents can get blindsided by facts and logic and miss the subtle changes that point out trouble.

There was no hard evidence to support Bec's mother's instincts at the time but later that night Bec's text messages revealed her mother was right. Her daughter had indeed had sex with a boy while she was meant to be at the corner store! Her father just couldn't believe that firstly he missed it and secondly, that he hadn't listened to his wife. How could he have not known that his daughter had been so deceitful?

My mother's favourite saying used to be, "You have to have eyes in the back of your head!"

Great parents realise how easy it is to miss stuff. Even the big stuff! There is no neon sign that spells out trouble. I have met the greatest of parents who have missed some incredible big stuff in their children's lives and it isn't because they didn't care. It is because they are blindsided by either a busy routine, ignorance, assumptions, or too much trust in their kids.

Adults very easily get caught up in their adult world. Sometimes they do not want to know what is going on in the lives of their teenagers. Adult-sized problems, like mortgages and work pressures, are things that take a slice of adult's time and attention. It is so important that we leave some room to perceive where our teenager is at.

We have to remember that it is what our daughters don't say rather than what they do that gives you the most insight into their lives. Great parents realise that it takes time and energy to use intuition to read between the lines. Great parents understand that it's natural for teenagers to keep them at an arm's length and they don't expect them to tell the truth. Great parents realise that teenagers are like icebergs: you see about 10 percent of what is really going on, and no matter how many questions you ask them, they are likely to always keep some things to themselves.

When parents ask, "How was school?" and their daughter answers, "Good," parents who don't exercise a lot of intuition are content with that answer. They assume that good means good. However, parents who use their intuition pay attention to the tone that was used, how long it took them to say the word good, their body language and whether they hesitated afterwards.

I encourage parents to respect their daughters' privacy rather than fight against it. Be content to not hear the details you would like to but instead realise you must rely on your intuition to fill in the gaps. Let's face it: trying to pry open a shut door will only lead to endless arguments in the home and make parents sound desperate for information! You don't have to know everything about your teenager's life to know how to parent them, especially if you use your intuition. In fact knowing everything probably won't change the way you parent at all.

Mums Write In...

YES, YES!! It's so easy to miss stuff!!! I consider myself to be a very alert parent but I can recall about three months ago when I spoke to her after her friend's mother told me her daughter said that my daughter had been crying herself to sleep for a few nights and she had been to the Beyond Blue website and rated herself as two points off high risk. Did I feel BAD! Why had I missed that??? I could bring up with her the specifics of what I knew and reveal that confidences had been broken but we had an emotional conversation in which she revealed to me that she felt really ugly. We both had a bit of a cry and I sometimes wonder if part of the reason she doesn't communicate is because she thinks I will get upset (or angry or be judgmental, or give her a lecture or be disappointed, or just not understand). After our discussion that night I kept a close eye on her and realised that she had been going through a low point and it was more typical teenage angst than true depression. I have since then discovered there was some 'friendship drama' going on in her group at around the same time so I think it is probably all tied in together. She is usually quite confident and is well liked amongst her peers but we're in Year 9 now so I am expecting that to all get turned on its head. You have to have eyes in the back of your head... literally!

STRATEGY 8:

Promote Self Defence

It's every parent's worst nightmare. Sexual assault does happen. Australian females aged 15-19 have the highest victimisation rate for sexual assault at a rate more than seven times the overall rate for sexual assault.[47] 28% of girls in secondary schools report having had unwanted sex[48].

I have sat with many girls after an incident of assault, often the day after, sometimes months after and other times years after. In many cases of abuse there were warning signs that were either ignored or went unnoticed. Fear is our body's natural way of warning us of danger. My concern is that most girls will not listen to their instincts because they haven't prepared themselves enough for the possibility of needing to protect themselves. It's important that our girls know that not everyone in the world is a safe person.

As parents it's essential to realise that teens or other children carry out a huge percentage of sexual abuse[49]. Society has been lulled into believing that children are at their core innocent. This coupled with ignorance about sexual development and the inclination for parents, educators and youth themselves to either deny or understate abusive incidents when they occur, leads to a huge issue[50], which no one seems to know how to address.

When there are complex circumstances, misunderstandings

or alcohol involved, it makes things really messy. At the end of the day 'no' means 'no', no matter when a girl said it or where she said it or how she said it. Of course drugs and alcohol and sex is never a good mix. If there are drugs and alcohol involved, sex should never be on the menu. Unfortunately, teenagers don't always get this memo.

I would want to know that my daughter could protect herself if she needed to. That is why I would love to see every girl enrol in a self-defence class as she hit puberty. If nothing else self-defence can build a huge amount of confidence in girls and give them the courage to listen to their gut feelings. It gives them a pre-warning that not everyone in the world has their best interests at heart, which I think is a really important lesson to learn.

You can't rehearse potential dangerous situations enough. Make it very clear to your daughter that if she feels uneasy for any reason, she should move as quickly as possible. That means she has to always be aware of the atmosphere around her. If it changes and she senses danger or feels fear she needs to be prepared to exit straight away. Gut instincts should never be ignored.

Nothing feels better than knowing you can take care of yourself mentally and physically. Being able to protect yourself in all situations is a confidence boost just as much as it is reassurance. Physical fitness and strength is also a great positive to have in your life that never goes astray.

Mums Write In...

When my daughter was 13, I thought it was a good idea to enrol her into a self-defence / karate type class. Little did I know that this was possibly a lifesaver for her only a few months later. We were on an overseas holiday and a man at the resort we were staying at approached her. It basically came down to attempted abduction and a lot of distress. It's always a good idea to teach your girls to get away whenever the need arises.

CHAPTER FOUR

Moods

A Snap Shot of Reality

Girls are hitting puberty earlier and earlier[51]. On average girls have their first period when they are around 12.5 years old but their bodies are changing and their breasts may start developing up to two years before this[52].

Anxiety disorders make up half of all mental illnesses in children and adolescents[53].

7.7% of 12-17 year old girls have a diagnosed anxiety disorder[54].

One in 20 Australian teenagers aged 12-17 has experienced a major depressive episode, and 1 in 14 has one or more anxiety disorders[55].

Roughly 10% of young people have self-harmed[56], and 12% of 13-17 year olds report having thoughts about suicide[57].

It is estimated that in the previous 12 months 298,000 Australian children and adolescents aged 4 -17 years would have had ADHD, 278,000 had anxiety disorders, 112,000 had major depressive disorder and 83,600 had conduct disorder[58]. Yet only one out of every four young persons with mental health problems had received professional health care[59].

Evidence suggests that half of adult mental health conditions emerge by age 14[60].

Australian primary schools have one of the highest reported rates of bullying in the world[61]. Around 1 in 4 children report being bullied every few weeks or more[62], and 10-20% of Australian children report having been cyberbullied[63].

The Story of Girls

I wanted to start this chapter off in a light-hearted way because there is no logic to fully explain the drama of a teenage girl. Laughter is the best medicine. If you think your daughter is a little off the Richter scale then you are not alone. I have asked a few mums of now young adult women to write in just to reassure you that your daughter is amongst a bunch of quality girls who have both lost the plot and grown through it.

When my now 22-year-old daughter was 13 I decided it would be special and exciting to take her to Myer for a trainer bra fitting. She was quite impressed that her newly blossoming boobies may need some holding up! Anyhow we get a specialist fitter lady in the Lingerie Department and she measures up Cassidy who by this stage has all sorts of ideas in her head about pretty new bras to wear. After some private measurements being taken the specialist lady announces that Cassidy's blossoming boobies have not blossomed enough for anything more than an exercise singlet!!! Cassidy promptly redresses, storms out of the change room and starts power walking through three floors of Myer with me in hot pursuit down escalators, two steps at a time! I finally catch her and explain that her time will come and apologise for her feelings of inadequacy because the adventure I had planned was meant for a happier outcome. Ten years later she has a wonderful selection of bras.

My middle daughter got very hormonal when she got her periods. One day she was walking home from a friend's house and she called me to say watch out, she's got her period and very grumpy. It was the responsible thing to do! I said, "Me too." As she got home and walked up the stairs we looked at each other and growled at the same time followed by a burst of laughter. I love this memory!

Many years ago my daughter threw cake mix at her brother because he called her a cutie. She then spent an hour in her room in tears. Her brother honestly thought he was giving her a compliment and didn't look at her for two days in fear of upsetting her again!

My funny story is about my now gorgeous 19 year-old who was at the time 15. She had run away from home. We were having a meeting with the school to choose her Year 11 classes. She was stuck at four electives she was happy with and needed one more to make up five. The principal suggested drama. She looked at him and then me and said, "Just because I am a drama queen doesn't mean I want to do drama!"

My solid as a rock child became a teenager overnight and would have moments when she would lose it, have a rant, stamp her foot and then let us have it. A few minutes later (literally a few minutes later) she would calmly shake her head and in her finest Queen's English say, "I am so sorry Mummy, I am not sure what came over me." It was like she was momentarily possessed. Thank goodness it only lasted about six months and she has well and truly grown through it.

I remember when my daughter was nearing her 15th birthday she said, "Mum I'm an emotional wreck!" When I asked her why (genuinely concerned), she said, "I'm getting old... I'm halfway to 30!" Dad then sympathetically chimed in and said, "Well my girl, consider this, I am halfway to 120."

It doesn't surprise me that girls struggle with their emotions so much. The teenage years are a time when our girls are trying to forge their own new identity. They are strongly committed to their new identity but it is still infantile and fragile. They know it can topple at any minute. They live with this sense of fragility every day.

They have a vision of being popular, pretty and smart (along with every other girl in their year level) but the daily grind of working this vision is hard work. They are surrounded by peers who are also fiercely committed to establishing their identity, which makes establishing their identity a competitive and messy process!

On top of all that teenagers have to deal with the physical changes that come with puberty. Although puberty and adolescence are related they are not the same thing[64]. As the body reaches puberty it kick starts neurobiological changes, however the body and the brain do not mature at the same rate. Even when the body has reached maturity the brain has a lot more work to do[65].

MRI studies show us that the brains of teenagers are very different to both those of children and those of adults[66]. Adolescence is not just a simple transition. It is a real, neurobiological transformation of the structures that control cognitive and emotional skills.

Throughout childhood the brain develops more and more connections, which send signals back and forth to help us interpret and understand the world around us. By the early teenage years the brain has accumulated the most connections it will have throughout our lifetime[67]. As the body reaches puberty the brain begins pruning back these connections, leaving only those that are determined to be the most important and focusing on improving and integrating these[68].

During teenage years thinking matures from focusing on the here and now to the ability to think abstractly, plan for the future and debate ideas[69]. Risk taking behaviours peak during puberty[70]. One of the later areas of the brain to mature is the prefrontal cortex, which regulates the ability to judge risk appropriately, control behaviour, regulate emotion and plan ahead[71]. This area of the brain is not completely mature until late adolescence or early adulthood[72].

With girls' bodies starting to go through pubertal changes at around 10 years old[73], it is no wonder that parents tell me that their primary aged girls are already acting like teenagers. They have a mix of pre-puberty hormones combined with a brain that is getting ready to cull[74]. Their bodies are starting to undergo changes and parents can see the mood swings and behaviour changes surfacing.

One parent I was speaking to yesterday, who had a 9 year-old girl told me of the erratic mood changes their daughter was displaying. One minute she was bubbly, over-affectionate and chirpy and then the next minute she was shut down and withdrawn. She had just invested hours into building a cubby house with her brother and then at a whim walked off and said "I don't want to do that now" and ended up crying in the corner about it. It was taking a lot of mum's time and patience to keep guiding this little girl.

Mum would sit down with her husband at night and analyse

her daughter's life, trying to work out if there was anything that could be impacting her. Could she be being bullied? Does she have any mental health issues starting to surface? Is she worried about her cousins who are going through a hard time? They even went to visit her teacher to ask the same questions. Nothing significant surfaced. They came to the conclusion that her hormones must be involved and they would have to, for now, put it down to pre-puberty.

In saying that we all know there are great differences between girls. In fact it is crazy how different two sisters can be! Some girls have relatively few emotional ups and downs while others seem to launch into another hemisphere. It's hard to definitively blame girls' outlandish behaviour on hormones, brain development, personality or evil genius. But without a doubt some girls struggle with their moods more than others.

The Teenage Brain

One of my young and talented psychologists shared with me her analogy of the teenage brain, which has helped me talk to parents about their daughters' emotions. It's a great example and for many parents explains why so many doors slam in their house over small issues. She asks parents to think of their daughters' brain like a three story building.

Level one is Airport Security, complete with men in uniform, laser guns and sniffer dogs. It only knows how to do one thing: determine whether the information incoming is a threat or not. If information is determined a threat the body's fight, flight, freeze system is activated. If there is no threat then the information is passed into the other levels of the brain. The only way we can determine if information is a threat or not is by consulting our memory bank. This helps us ascertain how we should respond.

Level 2 of the brain is the Limbic System. This is the emotional part of our brain. If the Limbic System had a stage name it would be Sasha Fierce. Like Sasha the Limbic system is loud, proud, SUPER expressive and not afraid to wear her heart on her sleeve. This is the part of the brain that slams doors, yells, cries, gets angry, has fierce opinions, becomes over-joyed, super excited and keeps us on our toes. When information gets to this level of the brain our girls ask themselves, "How do I feel about this?" and then they let the world know about it.

Level 3 is the Executive Functioning or Prefrontal Cortex. A great way to describe the Prefrontal Cortex is a boardroom or a committee of management, which analyses everything in detail. It looks at the information from every angle to help us make the best decision possible. When information gets to this level of the brain our girls ask themselves questions like, "Why do I feel like this? How can I best respond? When have I felt like this before? Do I need more information before I make another decision? Where is the best place to go to get more information?" And on and on...

Once information has passed through Level 1 of an adult's brain you can expect Level 2 and Level 3 to both engage in order to make a heartfelt and logical decision. Ideally, a brain spends 50% of its time in Level 2 and 50% of its time in Level 3. We need a balance of both to process life well. Not all adults'

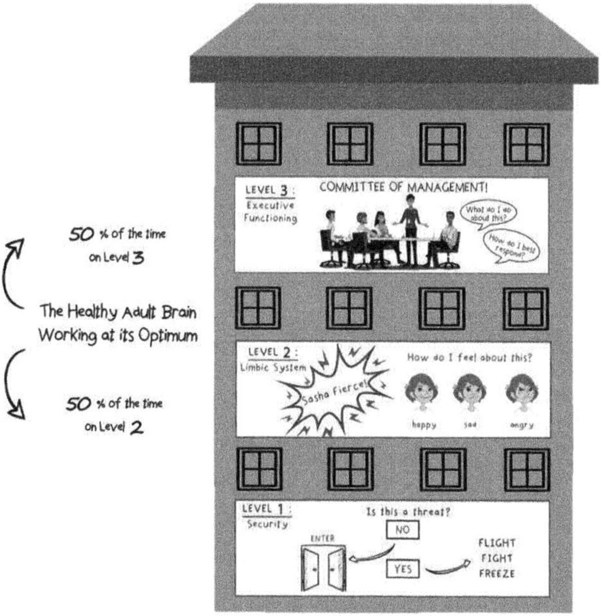

brains function with this much efficiency and brain health has a lot to do with how effectively the Limbic System and executive function areas interrelate. However this is the ideal.

This is the good bit, which I hope will help you heaps!

When our girls hit puberty, they go through a period where their brains prune back in order to function more efficiently[75]. You can liken it to your daughter culling her wardrobe after keeping all her clothes for 12 years. This is understandably a huge task for the brain. The brain has to delegate the leadership of this task to one of its three levels. Given Airport Security's (Level One) limited capacity, The Limbic System's (Level two) proven emotional outbursts and The Board Room's (Level three) superior analytical ability, the task is officially delegated to Level 3.

However this has a great impact on the teenage brain's day-to-day function. While the board members are busy with this task of sorting, reorganising and culling they have very little time to spend on day-to-day matters. That means that Sasha Fierce is left with the majority of the control when it comes to day-to-day decision making. Oh my! That explains a lot, doesn't it??! Perhaps that is why teenager girls slam so many doors! Research also tells us that executive functioning ability doesn't fully mature until at least the late 20s so the teenage years are not fully over when they turn 18[76].

A father told me a while ago that his daughter was screaming "I hate you" at the top of her lungs at him. He admitted to wanting to scream back, "I hate you too." I had to laugh. He was honest. Instead he had the presence of mind to override his emotions. He opted for this response, "I won't deny you

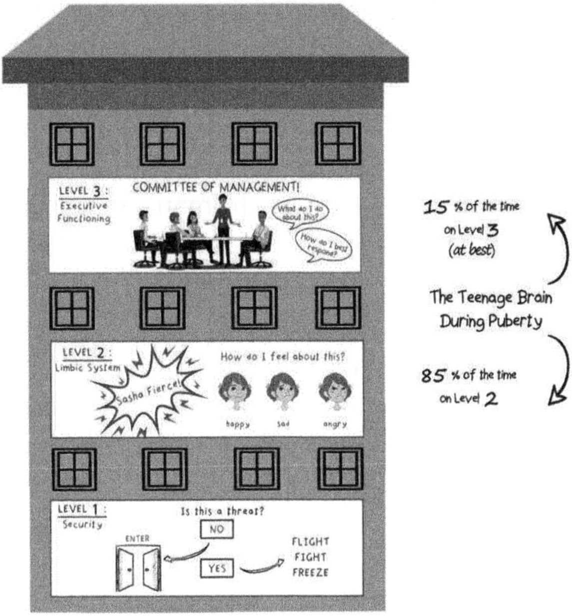

are annoying me no end right now but I don't have the right to hate you. I am your father and I will never hate you. I only have the right to love you." To which Sasha Fierce probably replied, "Whatever."

The best advice I can give you for this stage is this: your daughter may look like a mini adult but she is not a mini adult. She is a teenager. There is a big difference between the two. You have to expect her to act like a teenager and you have to expect to have to be her parent. Teenagers need parents to be their executive functioning during this stage of their life.

How We Can Truly Help

One mum likened her daughters who were struggling with moods like playing emotional twister. She never knew what emotional state her daughters were going to wake up in each morning. It usually depended on how little sleep they got the night before. "Some mornings were volatile," she told me. "If you even looked at them it was like the whole world was coming to an end. They erupted over the slightest things."

Living with a girl who has dramatic mood swings can be draining and demanding. It can take a toll on the whole family. I see parents cope in all different ways, not all which are healthy. Sometimes I see parents cope by becoming detached and withdrawn. I often see dads avoiding communicating because they don't think it will do any good. Dads tell me that when the tension rises in their home they leave it to their wives or partners and just exit the room. Like I have said in the introduction of this book, parents don't fight very hard against something they can't see themselves winning.

Another way I see parents cope is becoming overly involved and taking responsibility for things their daughters should be responsible for. Sometimes parents get overly involved because they feel the intensity of their daughters' pain and want to rescue them from it. Other times they don't want the backlash when things go wrong so they try and head it off at the gate.

One of my staff had a young lady who came into a counselling session crying, saying she couldn't handle life because her boyfriend's cat (who she had never met) died. Turned out that she had just started her period. This same week she had also decided she couldn't do a speech in front of the boys in her class. She had thrown a huge tantrum until mum called her teacher and arranged a special class session for only the girls to view her speech. In this girl's case, mum came to the rescue every time her daughter had a problem. This came from a good place but didn't allow the daughter to experience or regulate her own emotions.

The truth is that we can't actually control our daughters' responses to life's circumstances. I know we would love to!!! All we can do is empathise with her, support her and then give her the tools she needs to manage her emotions. She has to choose to use those tools. When she doesn't manage herself well it is easy to make excuses, blame others or manipulate the environment to change the outcome. It becomes exhausting when a mum won't let go and let life teach her daughter.

My greatest advice for parents of girls who struggle with their moods is allow them to make as many of their own decisions as possible. Then allow them to feel the consequences of their own choices. Life is the best teacher. We repeat behaviour that works for us. The earlier our daughters discover what works in real life the better opportunities they will have to develop resilience and grow. Sheltering them from their choices will only delay their growth.

STRATEGY 1:

Eliminate Health Issues

Today I had a beautiful 18 year-old girl in my office who was desperate to leave home. While her desire for independence was absolutely normal, her overall stability and health had to be considered. She was struggling with depression and in the middle of changing her medication. Her state of mind wasn't great and I am sure that was contributing to the fights she was having with her parents. Her parents were worried that another big change was going to tip her over the edge. Their perspective made me stand up and take note.

Teenagers' lives are full of big decisions. Some of these decisions will cause a ripple effect that will impact them for many years to come. We know that a healthy state of mind is the best platform for sound decisions. When girls aren't in a positive state of mind parents have good reason to be concerned. Sometimes parents can intervene and other times all they can do is hope and pray that their daughters will listen to a voice of wisdom.

There is a big different between mental illness and mental health. Mental illnesses are medical conditions that cause a significant change in the way a person thinks, behaves and interacts with other people[77]. Mental health is a state of wellbeing where every individual realises her own potential, can cope with the normal stresses of life and can work productively and make a positive contribution to their community[78].

Our girls need to recognise that their mental health is something that needs to be nurtured in order to be maintained and protected so they can function well and make sound decisions.

Nurturing something until it grows strong takes time. Sleep disturbances, self-harm, eating disorders, depression and anxiety are all significant issues that many of our girls face. However, many times these issues can be avoided with early intervention and appropriate self care.

Eliminating health issues is one of the first things I do when families have big concerns about their daughters' behaviour and ability to make sound decisions. Diagnosis can only be made by a professional, not at home using an online checklist found on a website. Remember too that the onset of puberty can exaggerate any existing medical conditions so it can be a confusing time for parents and their daughters.

Even once a diagnosis is made there is the ongoing challenge of determining what is mental illness and what is normal teenager behaviour and how to manage each. Bringing up a child who has OCD or chronic depression or even ADHD is a tough gig because you not only have to consider the normal aspects of puberty and adolescent development, you have to then consider aspects of an illness they can't control. Parents who have children who struggle with diagnosed depression often ask me how to manage chores and school attendance, not knowing when to make exceptions and when not to. This is often a fine line!

A good family doctor is a really underrated service. If you don't have a family doctor spend some time shopping around for one. Ask your friends, family and your daughter's school for their recommendations. Please remember that you can always talk to a doctor about any concerns you have in relation to your daughter's development including puberty, brain health and moods. If they can't help you they can refer you to someone who will.

Mums Write In...

I'm not sure if it's because of my personality or evil genius but I may or may not have been responsible for punching / kicking more than one hole in the walls of my parents' home when in high school that only got fixed around the time I hit my thirties. For many years mum used my actual high school artwork to cover one of my wall-kicking 'artworks' and I can neither confirm nor deny that I once overturned a monopoly game and stormed out of the house in my early twenties. Look how far I have come! And I was considered a normal child!

STRATEGY 2:

Teach Self Care

Knowing how to manage emotions and comfort yourself when you are unhappy or distressed is a skill that can take anyone a long time to learn. Even grown women look for someone else to comfort and rescue them! Why? Because it takes self-perception to find strategies that truly work, especially because we are always growing and evolving as human beings.

How we self-care changes according to the stage of life that we are in? Self-care for a two year old is very different to self-care for a 12 year-old and a 30 year-old. Renegotiating what your self-care looks like in each stage of your life requires a reassessment of what is working and what is not working. Self-care requires you look at your entire life to discover what you need next. It takes foresight.

Because our daughters are prone to looking externally instead of looking internally they often copy the self-care strategies of others. They may look at what the reality TV stars do or what their friends do. I find that girls' down time is often spent wishing they were someone else, or somewhere else, instead of truly nurturing themselves and being honest about who they are and what fills them with joy.

We can get stuck seeing our teenagers like children and not allowing them the opportunity to explore self-care strategies for themselves. I find that mums try and manage this area of their daughter's lives. I hear mums say, "If they are going to act like a child I am going to treat them like a child." Unfortunately, what worked for them as a child won't work for them as a teenager, regardless of their childish behaviour. We might offer them the self-care strategies that used to work for them when they were younger, like staying home to rest or going out as a family. Yet dictated methods of self-care seldom work. Self-care strategies work because they bring reward or perceived reward.

During puberty our daughters have to experiment and find new ways of coping. As parents we have to be flexible in allowing this process to happen. Sometimes we are too rigid and hold on to what worked for us when our daughters were young. We can be working with the old game book even when our daughters have written several updated editions. Cut them some slack. Long periods of time in their bedroom are a normal part of self-discovery, as may also be them wanting to socialise all the time.

In saying all that, I see great value in our girls participating in self-care strategies that they may not currently identify with. Families may deliberately work self-care into their family's daily routine for everyone's benefit. For example, setting aside time to talk, cooking healthy food together, or exercising together. Adding self-care strategies into a family routine enables girls to broaden their self-care skills and adopt strategies that may be different than their own.

Emotions demand movement. Emotions move our bodies and our thoughts in all sorts of ways. However, we have to be careful where they move us. The trick is finding healthy ways to move. Here are some self-care strategies that girls may benefit from:

Comforting - Hugging a teddy, playing with a stress ball, cuddling a soft blanket, candlelight and taking a warm bath are all things that engage the senses and calm us down. They may seem like trivial things but they really do help.

Creating - Colouring In, drawing, making things with play-dough, writing letters or playing music all provide a way for girls to regulate their emotions. For gifted creative people, music may be their lifeline. For others, keeping a diary is something that is central to their daily self-care.

Socialising – Going to the movies, helping someone else, going to a public place and hanging with people you care about. Some girls really do need to connect with people in order to unwind so don't dismiss the importance of a good laugh, people contact and some entertainment.

Constructive Thinking – Balancing out the emotional brain with some logic can be really powerful. No girl tells their friends that they actually go home and talk to their mother but the reality is that confident teenagers have hidden support. Mums, be careful that you aren't starting deep conversations at 10pm when they should be shutting their brains down and getting ready for bed. Set aside talking time earlier in the night, say 7pm, so it's done and dusted by 9pm and they can get ready to unwind.

Organising – Reorganising your room, clothes, books, photos or even building something can be so soothing for some girls.
I have met some girls that the moment they feel overwhelmed they go straight to sorting out their bedrooms.

Moving – The benefits of movement can't be ignored. Even if your daughter isn't sporty, going for a walk everyday will do them the world of good. Moving together as a family is such a great thing to do. Exercise will help them relieve stress and clear their mind if practised regularly. Going for a bike ride, going to the gym, punching a punching bag, boxing, self-defence, dance and swimming are all great ways to move.

Quiet Time - Most people have a collection of things they do by themselves when they are feeling down. These things may include watching television, playing computer games, listening to music, cooking or reading. Positive distractions will help them re-balance. Negative distractions may work in the opposite way. The challenge with teenagers is they tend to gravitate to negative things when they feel negative.

Meditation - Meditation is a lost art in our society. Some people use relaxation music to purposefully empty their minds. Yoga and mindfulness are all tools that our girls can use to focus their energy. Sitting and doing nothing will work well too. Girls need some quiet time, often alone, just to let their mind relax, refresh and get some time out.

Mums Write In...

Yes, yes, yes! I always knew there was a reason that my family routine kept my girl grounded. We have movie nights with our kids. Sometimes we pull out the wedding video, pop some popcorn and pull up the beanbags. My kids love camping and there is nothing that relaxes them more. It's like it brings them back to basics. We pull out the tents and sleeping bags, pack the marshmallows and head off together. The amount of children who have never been camping (outside of school camp) is astounding. I've heard mums say, "My idea of camping is a mattress on the floor of the Sheraton!" "What, I say?? Kids love camping!!! According to Roy Morgan research, June 2015, just 12% of Australian travellers 14+ years reported camping in a tent on their last holiday ahead of people who travelled as a family with kids at only 10.9%.

STRATEGY 3:

Don't Make Excuses for Her

Hypersensitivity is common to teenage girls. Research agrees by telling us that the Limbic System is three times as active during adolescence as any other time in their lives. Parents are often compensating for this hypersensitivity by providing additional support and care. However, we can over do it and run the risk of raising girls who are weak, emotionally stunted and unable to solve their own problems.

I notice that a lot of parents I work with perceive their children as fragile and in need of protection from negative feelings. They get worried that saying no to their girls will cause emotional damage. They fear tipping their child over the edge or damaging them by coming down too hard. I'm not sure this is a good place to parent out of.

Clara and her dad get along well except for times when Clara feels that dad picks on her. Her dad might say, "Clara don't do it like that. Do it like this." Instead of taking it as intended, Clara bursts into tears and feels attacked. Her oversensitivity makes her dad's eye roll. Mum knows dad intended no harm but defends Clara nonetheless. Mum expects dad to change his tact in order to not upset Clara. Clara's emotional state is the number one priority.

Mums, it is very common for us to become overprotective of our daughters. We can end up blaming other people when in fact our girls need to take more responsibility for their responses. The real world won't tip-toe around our kids like we do. And although we don't want to deliberately trigger them into a meltdown we can't blame each other or cocoon them in fantasy-land. We have to act normally around them. Perhaps our daughters need to adjust rather than the world adjusting for them.

Mums, I want to reassure you of this. She can handle it! That means no cooking a special meal for her because she will throw a tantrum if she is served roast beef. That means no blaming her brother for not framing his language in a particular way. You have to have full confidence in her that she is strong enough to cope with the things life throws at her. She can handle it. We must back our girls and believe in their ability to overcome whatever they are facing, whether that is anxiety, depression, bullying or finding the right career paths. Yes, we might have to guide and encourage them but I have full confidence they will find their way.

Our girls need to know it is their responsibility to regulate their own emotions. That means we have to let go and let them learn. I can't emphasise how important this is for their emotional maturity and resilience. Parents can struggle with the letting go process. After all they have always been the source of comfort for their children.

That doesn't mean we turn into heartless and distant parents. We are always there if they are unsafe. We will always protect them. What we must do is define the difference been unsafe and unhappy. I say it like this. Give your daughter the appropriate amount of attention for situations so you don't run the risk of dramatising or becoming over involved in things she needs to be working out herself.

This is an analogy I use often. When she was young and scratched herself while playing she would cry, you would rub it, maybe put a band-aid on it and then you would encourage her to stop crying and get on with her day. If you have the same response to scratch size teenage issues you will be parenting her well. Give the problem an appropriate amount of attention. Show you care and then put the ball in her court because you are confident she can handle it.

We all had to learn to manage our emotions. Resilience isn't just a word on posters around schools. It is something that needs to be worked out in our girls' lives on a daily and weekly basis in order for them to be able to reach their dreams. It starts day in, day out allowing our girls to work their muscles as they face life's challenges. It also starts with us as parents letting go.

Mums Write In...

Thanks for chatting earlier Michelle. So we had three meltdowns before we even got into the car, but I tried very hard not to make excuses – gee that was difficult! But I feel strongly that my daughter has to start taking responsibility for her emotions. It's really hard to see her struggling to sort herself out. I'll have to listen to my husband, who doesn't sugar coat anything and says it like it is. I know she is only nine but I can see if I don't get on top of things now I am going to have big trouble. There are a couple of times when she has walked down the street to calm down this week. She comes back less angry. She doesn't come back happy but calmer. I have told her that she can't do that because I can't see her. I know that she has a little diary in her room that she uses sometimes. If she is really mad she goes to her room and does something like writing, drawing or playing with toys. It works to a certain degree - as long as I keep her younger brother away from her!

STRATEGY 4:

Check the Schedule

Life in the fast lane of the 21st century is busy. The constant, continual pace of academics, extra curricular activities, part-time jobs and the dings of phones make for an action-packed life. The greatest challenge is for our girls to find the time to care for themselves and place priority on what gives them strength as a person. That is hard to do with a phone in your hand 24/7. It is also hard to do when you are comparing yourself to reality television stars and celebrities who don't live realistic lives. Our girls live in a world of perceived perfection, and many of them are literally falling apart while trying to keep up.

I have been astounded at what some family's schedules look like and what they perceive to be a normal routine. I have often had families come to see me for anxiety-related issues and when I see their weekly routine I start to have a panic attack myself. There is no way I would be able to keep up the pace! There is no time to eat, let alone sleep! Some of our girls are high achievers yet we still need to make sure they have some down time to process their awesomeness!

I definitely see anxiety overtaking our girls' lives. Anxiety disorders make up half of all mental illnesses in children and adolescents[79] 7.7% of 12-17 year-old girls have a diagnosed anxiety disorder[80]. Unfortunately it is a real issue for this generation and I encourage parents to look out for the warning signs. One of those signs can simply be over activity.

Anxiety can produce over activity, but the problem with over-activity is that it usually produces more anxiety. We can stay up all night worrying about something that has no merit only to find that it produces more stress in our upcoming day. Activity for activity sake doesn't help. We need to make sure our girls are intentionally choosing safe and wise ways to channel any anxious feelings.

It's a good idea to assess our daughter's schedule each term, as it may need to change in the light of how she is physically, emotionally and socially coping. Check how well she is eating. Food is essentially medicine. Our daughters' diets are a critical factor in the management of their moods. Excessive sugar, caffeine and white carbohydrates are known to de-stabilise mood, as does irregular eating. Energy drinks containing caffeine have a huge impact on our teenagers' moods. When our daughters skip breakfast and replace it with a coffee or an energy drink, they de-stabilise their mood from the very beginning of the day.

Keep an eye on the amount and quality of sleep your daughter is getting. This is a critical factor in enabling her mood to stabilise. Having an uninterrupted nine hours of sleep is something that is so important to the health of teenagers, but very rare. If they do miss out on sleep, the weekends are a great time to catch up. A teenager who consistently has difficulty sleeping should seek professional support because it is so critical for their mental health.

When anxiety kicks in self-care gets squeezed out of the schedule. That's the time when our daughters' rooms get messy, their diets get poor, their sleep cycles get muddled up and their moods get crazy. Parents: on a side note, it might not be a bad idea to your check own schedule and stress levels from time to time. Our anxiety can make quite an impression on our kids!

Another thing I make sure I do is acknowledge how scary anxiety makes a girl feel. However, I try and acknowledge it without making it more frightening or dwelling on it. That means I might say, "This is really scary for you, isn't it? But I have seen you get through this before." Or I might say, "I can feel how scared you are right now, but you are safe and you have a plan to go forward." That way we are empathising without contributing to the fear. It also models the internal dialogue that they can use to support themselves. This has nothing to do with schedules, but I thought I'd throw it in any way!

Mums Write In...

My 14 year-old is always asking to have a 'Mother' drink or 'V' drink. She says all her friends drink them. It really annoys me that shops can sell these drinks. I have told her of the health problems associated with them, like increased heart rate and increased chance of developing addictions to drus, as she gets older. The problem is the other kids do it and I actually have seen parents buying it for such young children and wonder why they are bouncing off the ceilings or arguing with them later. Fortunately she is a very focused sportswoman so she knows that this is not a good choice for her. Maybe parents should take this approach and turn it around to make it seem as if it is a bad choice for the teenager. They all have something that they are good at. Just redirect this choice around them.

STRATEGY 5:

Hit and Run Praise

Don't be fooled by your daughter's diminished desire for parental affirmation. She still needs you on her team. Our affirmation may be the only praise she hears amongst the bombardment of judgements and criticisms she encounters from those her own age. Have you heard how harsh the school yard banter can be these days?

Parents of 15 year-olds tell me that their daughters' self-talk and conversation at home are negative and full of complaining, especially when things aren't right with their friendships. One mother explained it like this, "These sassy snaps are a horrible way to relate to one another but her only way to survive. It seems to be a way that girls protect themselves from the drama. It's dark humour. Underneath you can see how hurt they are."

I suggest parents introduce a different type of snap. Turn up out of nowhere. Hit them with praise and then run. You can hit your daughters with comments like, "I love you"; "You look great in that shirt"; "Gosh you are working hard"; "You are going to make a great mum one day" and then run. Get out of there. You can hit them with a compliment when you are passing them in the hallway when they are getting out of the car, when they are leaving the house. Don't wait around to see them roll their eyes or tell you that you sound stupid. Hit and then run. Swoop in and get out of there before they have time to have a go at you.

Another really practical way to incorporate respectful language is introducing a Respect Chart. The idea is for each member of the family to write one thing they respect about the other members of the family on the chart each day. When it doesn't come naturally sometimes you have to deliberately schedule it in. I have seen this work really well in blended families or families where the respectful language has been missing for long periods of time. It does work better for families who have some younger members to drive its enthusiasm.

Our Respect Chart

	Monday	Tuesday	Wednesday	Thursday	Friday	Saturday	Sunday
Sammie	You were kind to your sister - Mum						
	You let me sit in the front seat - Kaitlin						
Kaitlin	You are fun ☺ - Sammie						
	You emptied the Dishwasher for me - Mum						
Mum	You cooked for me - Kaitlin						
	You always ask me how I am - Sammie						

Mums Write In...

On a personal note, I'm still struggling with the communication aspect. I get how important it is but it doesn't come easily to me and my teenager who just clams up, tells me "nothing is wrong"; "everything is okay"; "no, she doesn't need or want to talk"; and all usually accompanied by a fair bit of eye rolling and arm crossing. I try to ask open questions or just be there for her when or if she needs to talk, but she often dismisses any concerns I may raise about hot topics (eg. bullying, virtual or actual sex and appropriate behaviour, appropriate online behaviour, etc.) by saying things like, "We talk about this all the time in PD at school" and is reluctant to commit to much more than that. She just has that 'can I go now?' look on her face and I feel as though she thinks I'm prying. I thought we had laid some good ground work in the earlier years so that communication would not be an issue, but for some reason it is a real struggle. So if you have any suggestions for that one let me know!! Is this just me or do other parents raise this issue with you?

STRATEGY 6:

Post Cat Videos

Every girl in the room identifies with it. The headaches they get when their friendship circle is having another meltdown. The uncertainty of not knowing whom to sit with at lunchtime. The gossip that leaves them speechless and the worry they will be the next victim. I certainly wouldn't want to be a teenage girl again.

There is a fine line between bullying and girl drama. I see some horrific cases of bullying which would make your stomach sick! We all know what to do about bullying on this scale. Or I hope you do! However, what do we do about the everyday girl dramas that consistently and relentlessly surround our girls' lives? How we do minimise the drama and make sure our girls aren't turning a bad day into a disaster by over-reacting to its situations they could have easily diffused?

Each day after school Alice would receive text messages from one of her close friends. Her friend would particularly want to gossip about another girl in their grade. Alice felt uncomfortable about it but didn't want her friend to think she didn't like her or wasn't prepared to listen to how she felt. Alice was caught between accommodating her friend and listening to her own conscious. What should she do?

I always recommend that girls don't try to correct someone their own age. They aren't their parents and they aren't their teacher. Being the boss of your peer never works when you are 13. So I asked her this, "What does your friend like?"

"She likes cats. She loves those funny cat videos," Alice replied.

"Okay every time she starts talking mean I want you to say, 'It'll blow over in a few days', and then send her a funny cat video. I want you to see what happens when you distract the whole situation."

I asked Alice to gather about 30 of the best funny cat videos she could find so she was super prepared.

And guess what? It worked. She kept her friendship intact and she also moved the conversation away from its current ugliness. I think her friend got the hint in a subtle and fun way.

I think it is necessary to continually talk to our girls about avoiding unnecessary drama. Being nasty will always backfire and destabilise their mood. When friendship dramas explode, encourage them to step back from the fire until the flame goes out. I often find myself writing 'I never do' statements with girls and asking mums to talk to their daughters about these concepts:

- I never bitch about another person online, even if we are fighting.
- If gossip starts I exit the conversation.
- If I feel uncomfortable I stop and ask myself why?
- I don't respond to trash talk or online bullying.
- I don't tell secrets online... nothing is secret.
- I think before I write.
- If in doubt I say nothing.
- I don't discuss personal problems online.

Mums Write In...

Friendship dramas are a definite trigger for mood swings in my girl! My daughter starts yelling for no reason and can even run out of the house and go and sit at the end of the driveway. On these days you know that anything will set her off so everyone keeps out of her way. The jobs go out the window and the huffing and puffing come out, or she starts lying. I guess the good news is that home is a safe place for our daughter to vent her frustrations! Like you said Michelle, I would hate to be a teenage girl again! The other day my daughter wrote something to another girl online, which I didn't think was really that bad at all! She was just sticking up for another girl and mentioned that bully word. This girl printed out the FB screen, showed the principal and she was suspended... This is an example of how FB comments (even if they are only slightly condemning) can blow up in your face! I can't talk to her enough about avoiding the drama because I don't want her to bring it home.

STRATEGY 7:

Respond to Self-Harm

I have worked with teenagers who self-harm for about 15 years. Over that time I have heard people cast a lot of judgement about young people who are self-harming. Some of the most common judgements I hear include, "If they actually wanted to kill themselves they would just do it"; "They are just ruining their body"; "They need to toughen up"; "Everyone has issues"; "They just want attention." If I ever start to judge a young person for self-harming I deliberately reframe my mind. Yes they are seeking attention, but for whatever reason they need it. I need to take care of them so they can learn to take care of themselves.

Self-harm is one of those topics that doesn't connect easily with us as an older generation. It's counter to 'the toughen up' culture so many of us were brought up with. So our default reaction is often subconsciously shaming, blaming and criticising - not because we don't want to help but because we don't know how else to handle it. Regardless of how widespread or mainstream self-harm has become it remains an issue which is difficult for many adults to fully understand. It takes time, deliberate effort *and often personal experience* to understand self-harm. I notice that adults who '*get it*' have usually made a concerted effort to do so. Those who don't limit their ability to be proactive in caring for young people.

The ways young people self-harm are wide and varied. They

are different and unique to each person. There are certainly differences between the tendencies of males and females and degrees to which young people self-harm. Although research definitely suggests that the most common form of self-harm is cutting followed by overdose[81], some of the forms of self-harm, which are less recognised, are: burning, self-battery, jumping from a dangerous height, stopping medication, freezing, strangling, suffocating, overdose, swallowing a non-ingestible object, train surfing, driving at high speeds and deliberate unsafe sex.

Research consistently tells us that the most common self-harm scenario involves a female with low level, with surface cuts on the skin horizontal rather than diagonal in nature. The incident takes place at home and she decided to harm in the hour before doing so. She deliberately hides the problem and is very sensitive talking about it. It is usually only picked up by someone close to her. There is often a close link between self-harm and depression[82].

I am seeing more and more parents concerned about pre-teens self-harming so I want you to know that they are never too young to start to self-harm. Teachers and parents alike tell me of little children who deliberately hit themselves, scratch themselves or cut themselves to express self-hatred or relieve strong emotions. For this reason all parents need to know the warning signs of self-harm:

- Knowledge of others who are self-harming.
- Unexplained marks on body.
- Wearing long sleeves that are never removed.
- Wearing wide wrist bands that are never removed.
- Difficulty expressing emotions.
- Secretive behaviour and/or extended time alone.

- Self-hatred.
- Items that could be used for cutting (sharpener blades, knives, scissors, safety pins, razors) missing.
- Signs of depression: withdrawn, sad, negative, lack of resilience.

Messages like these also teach me a lot about self-harm and how families cope with it:

Michelle, my daughter was self-harming and I had no idea how to handle it. As I researched I found it hard to find useful information. I took her to a counselling centre but it didn't help much. I understood why she was doing it on a technical level but I still couldn't get my head around why she would want to hurt herself. I physically hurt when I saw cuts on her arm and body. I would feel sick to the stomach and go into panic. There were times when she needed stiches. It was horrible. We decided to do regular checks of her room to take away devices that she would use to cut and keep the house safe until she was in a better headspace. This affected the whole family. I learnt the best thing to do was not to react when she self-harmed. I also got counselling to help me cope. I hope this helps someone else out there going through it.

It is extremely difficult for many parents to understand self-harm let alone know how to respond to self-harm, so I always suggest they get some professional help. Here is a starting point to help parents respond well to self-harm:

- Breathe. Breathe. Breathe. Give yourself a minute.
- Don't judge, assume or shame the young person.
- You might start that conversation by saying, "I am concerned about you. I'd like to talk to you about what is going on" ; or "I'm here if you want to talk more about this."

- Don't focus on the self-harm. Focus on self-care.
- Don't keep bringing up the topic of self-harm unless they want to talk about it.
- Speak positively into their future.
- Keep as many positives in their lives as possible.
- Commit for the long haul.
- Get some professional support for them AND for you.
- Process your emotions away from your teenager.
- Suicide and self-harm are often unrelated but a professional will be able to determine their safety if you are concerned.

Mums Write In...

My daughter used to self-harm. She would tell me that the pain on her skin made her forget about the pain on the inside. She would take the blades out of razors and hide them in rooms. Once a boy in her class said to her, "Why don't you go cut yourself?" and she was really hurt by that comment. As a mum it made me feel quite helpless at times. I didn't understand why she was doing it. She would come up with textbook answers things she had read online. At the time it seemed like everyone was doing it and it was a fad. I often wonder if she just joined in the bandwagon and started believing the words she was saying as she went along. Then for her it became something she couldn't stop. When she hurt herself I told her to make sure she cleaned it to stop it getting infected. I tried not to give her too much attention over it hoping she would stop, as she wasn't getting the reaction she wanted. Hindsight is a terrible thing. If I had my time over I would get some professional help sooner.

STRATEGY 8:

Be Fun

As adults we often walk around with the weight of the adult world on our shoulders and we don't have time or interest in childish things. Our schedules are jam packed with adult pressures and cares. As a result we get boring. When both mums and daughters, or dads and daughter (or heaven forbid mums, dads and daughters) are all stressed it's a recipe for disaster.

One mum told me the funniest story ever! She had a big fight with her daughter while she was on holiday and when they reached a car park (at the shopping centre) her daughter jumped out of the car and started to run away. The mum was so scared because she didn't know the area and she knew her daughter didn't either. When her daughter was about 100 meters away she yelled at the top of her voice, "I've got my periods!" Her daughter stopped immediately and returned saying, "Gosh, why didn't you tell me sooner. I would have understood why you were so grumpy. That makes so much sense." Then mum said, "Only joking!" They both cracked up laughing. She really knew the power of a good laugh.

Answer these questions for me honestly right now:

- Are you enjoying your kids?
- Are they enjoying you?
- When was the last time you had a good laugh with them?
- When was the last time you did something unexpectedly exciting?

- When was the last time you planned something as a family that everyone enjoyed?

It takes hard work to stay on the fun side of the island but when we do it goes a LONG way. Keeping our mood positive can help balance out our daughters' moods.

Mums Write In...

Please, please MAKE my husband read THIS! He thinks he is teaching my daughter to take responsibility by standing beside a light switch and telling her to come (from the other end of the house) to turn it off because she was the last one in that room. The result – A BIG argument! My thoughts – aren't there more important things to be lecturing her about? If you've been doing it for five years and it's not working I think it's a lost cause. I've decided not to pull him up on every little thing like that because every time I open my mouth it would be to nag about something which, in the overall scheme of things, is really just not that important. My husband can't seem to separate picking up the bath mat from her borrowing countless sums of money! I wish he'd save his energy for the important things and just relax a little and have some fun. PS. Darling I love you!

CHAPTER FIVE

Drugs and Alcohol

A Snap Shot of Reality

In 1999, 1 in 10 twelve -17-year-olds reported never drinking alcohol, but in 2014, this increased to 1 in 3 reported never drinking alcohol[83].

Some of the reasons for this dramatic decrease include religious or cultural beliefs, sporting or academic goals, family history of misuse, don't like the taste or don't like the cost.[84]

Despite this, young people identified alcohol and drugs as the top issue facing Australia today[85].

80.9% of teenagers have drunk alcohol by age 15, and 90.1% have drunk alcohol by age 17[86].

The average age for Australian teenagers to start drinking is 15.7[87].

20% of Australians aged between 14 and 17 are binge drinkers[88], meaning they consume more than five standard drinks in a drinking episode.

Those who begin drinking before age 14 are significantly more likely to develop abuse problems[89]. Those who start drinking earlier are also more likely to use alcohol to cope with difficult emotions, conflict with others and physical discomfort[90].

Teenage girls are binge drinking significantly more than previous generations[91].

Young women who use drugs at age 18 are more likely to have an unplanned pregnancy before age 29[92].

More than 95% of young people have never used illicit drugs with the exception of cannabis[93]. 82.4% report never using cannabis[94].

The Standard Teenage Experience

"Celina's parents let her drink alcohol."

"I don't care what Celina's parent do. You're my responsibility. I don't think fourteen year-olds should be drinking alcohol."

"I wish I had Celina's mother. Celina's mother is cool."

Great. It's official. You aren't cool. Your kid would rather live with someone else and what started out as a nice night was about to finish disastrously. But you know you are making the right decision, regardless of what your daughter tells you every other parent is doing. Buddying up to your kid and buying them adult 'supplies' just doesn't seem to be right. You have to be the parent rather than the friend.

But you know that not every parent shares this opinion. There are a lot of different ideas and values out there when it comes to alcohol use. I personally meet many parents who think experimenting with alcohol is a pretty standard teenage experience. Doing drugs on the other hand is the stuff that completely freaks parents out. Alcohol is the grey area.

I have met parents who have thrown their daughter a 14th birthday party and have supplied three beers each for her eighty friends. I have met other families who think it is wrong to supply alcohol to other people's kids but think it is okay for their daughter to drink at a family gathering. I have met very few parents who have an absolutely 'no alcohol until you are 18' policy for their teenagers.

The only way I can get my head around all this is to accept that alcohol is entrenched in our culture. It is not a new issue like social media. The use and misuse of alcohol has been around for generations. Our concepts about alcohol are driven by years of seeing and experiencing alcohol in our families and communities. Perhaps because we are so familiar with alcohol we tend to ignore the risks it has on a developing brain.

Medical experts now say there is no safe or recommended amount of alcohol for a teenager to drink because even one drink can do the growing brain some damage. Alcohol particularly affects the hippocampus and the prefrontal area of the brain, both which undergo major changes during adolescence. If a young person is going to drink alcohol make sure it is in small amounts and that they don't drink regularly. According to research teenagers should not be drinking alcohol at all.

Parents shouldn't forget the liver. Alcohol is the liver's worst enemy. The liver is the largest internal organ and is not yet functional enough in a child under eighteen to metabolise and excrete the toxins produced by alcohol sufficiently, resulting in lower thresholds for toxicity. Girls also have a lower threshold than boys. In general the consensus is that alcohol and teenagers should not mix.

The Partying Culture

Partying has become a major part of our teenagers' world. It dominates many schoolyard conversations. I hear endless chatter about what they are going to wear, how much they are going to drink, who they are going to hook up with and where they are going to crash for the night. Teenagers carefully plan for the next moment they are going to be free to have fun.

Parents need to understand that in a teenagers' world one drink quickly leads to another. There are very few teenagers who know how to drink responsibly, especially in a high-pressure partying environment. And there is no doubt that when alcohol is in the hands of teenagers there is often abhorrent misuse of it.

Media images of teenagers slamming down drink after drink in record time seems to shock adults. Parents seem to be able to get their heads around teenagers drinking alcohol responsibly but not teenagers binge drinking and passing out, which is usually closer to the reality I see. I notice that females who are drunk seem to horrify people a lot more than drunken males! Why? The risks appear to be much higher. Girls who binge drink put themselves at risk of sexual assault, being the target of gossip, car accidents, passing out, spewing everywhere, physical abuse and doing things they will completely regret.

Safety is a huge factor when it comes to alcohol consumption. I personally can't understand why parents would allow their daughters to mix foolishness with foolishness... I mean don't teenagers already take enough risks without the introduction of alcohol? There are so many stupid things a teenager can do when they have consumed too much alcohol. They have the rest of their lives to drink responsibly. Is it really necessary to introduce it at fourteen?

The Non-Negotiable Line

I can't talk about alcohol without touching on drugs. They are dangerous, illegal, and yes, they are everywhere. You don't have to go looking for them anymore. You can expect that if your teenager is at a party not only will alcohol pop up but so will drugs. And now that you are freaking out (because drugs freak all parents out). Take a deep breath. Just because drugs are in your teenager's reach doesn't mean your daughter will take them. A lot of teenagers don't take them simply because they understand they are harmful in a big, big way. We can't underestimate the importance or impact that education actually has. Research tells us that we are winning as far as drugs and teenagers go.

Statistics show that 4.8% of 12-13 year-olds have tried marijuana, which rises to 26.7% of 16-17 year-olds[95]. Around one in five 12-13 year-olds have deliberately sniffed inhalants and around 1.4% have tried amphetamines[96]. The number of Australians using methamphetamine, or ice, is the highest it has ever been. The rate of 15-24 year-olds using methamphetamine has doubled over the past five years, with 1.5% of this age group reporting dependent use of methamphetamine[97].

The one drug that teenagers are very likely to come across in high school is marijuana[98]. In some schools principals tell me that up to two thirds of their students smoke marijuana casually. Unfortunately in many circles, marijuana is seen as a harmless recreational drug. There are so many ups with smoking marijuana that is it so difficult for teenagers to see the down side. However I see the end result of teenagers who have used marijuana for long periods of time and believe me, there is a down side.

Marijuana is a depressant so it slows down the body. This feeling of calm can be really addictive if your daughter is feeling anxious or experiencing a stressful period in life. Heavy use of marijuana has the potential to damage the brain permanently. Teenagers who smoke marijuana become slow, lifeless and brain dead. The legal implications are real too. Convictions can damage their employment and travel opportunities. Marijuana is alongside of alcohol, the second biggest issue you need to be concerned about.

Drugs interact with the developing brain differently than they do with a fully developed adult brain. That is why teenagers get hooked on drugs so quickly. Drugs can so quickly replace any other positive activity in a teenagers' life. I find this the most difficult thing to watch. It frustrates me no end to see a talented, capable sports person throw it all way for the next joint. Instead of thinking about applying for a job or even getting up for school the next morning, all they think about is the next party and the next bong or hit. The scariest thing about drugs is that they steal potential, and let's face it, potential is all most teenagers have got going for them when they are fourteen.

And the worst part: where can a lack of purpose and a lot of alcohol and drugs lead teenagers? It can lead them into a life of crime. When teenagers are intoxicated they are more likely to do really silly, silly things like break into a house and steal CDs worth like a few hundred dollars. Real organised crime! The whole thing can get mixed up really quickly, so my advice is to take the hard line against drugs as early as possible. Get in hard and quick because drugs can take hold in a blink of an eye!

The Family Back Pack

I think the most important thing to address when it comes to alcohol (and drugs) and cigarettes and all addictive substances for that matter is how we handle them as adults. I see so many families who go through tough times (like a divorce or money troubles) and the first thing they turn to is the bottle, which usually leads to fights within the home and then more drinking. Although we all know there are better ways to handle stress our culture is so entrenched in a misuse of alcohol that many of us don't blink twice at this scenario.

I hope you can open your heart and mind as I get really honest and share an example with you that has changed my understanding of parenting. It is an example that has stayed with me throughout many years of my life. It really helps me make tough decisions and be a responsible adult during those times when I'd rather be a kid myself.

Here it is....

I want you to imagine a backpack.

It is a family backpack. It has been in your family for generations, passed down from one generation to the next. This backpack holds in it everything that your family represents : their values, skills, assets, character traits, experiences and ideals.

Some of the items in your backpack will be very positive, while others may not be as positive. Your backpack may hold the values of hard work, discipline, security and faith. It may also hold abuse, neglect, bankruptcy, broken relationships or addictions. The combination of both negative and positive items represents the reality of life and the choices of adults who have gone before you.

You don't get to choose what is in your backpack so unpacking the backpack is both an exciting and nervous moment for each generation. The items you find provide you with an important starting point in life. The more positive items you find the more opportunities you have in front of you. The more negative items you find the more challenges you will face.

However the most exciting thing about your family backpack is that it comes with one golden opportunity. When you have it in your possession you may alter its contents by adding or subtracting items. The addition or subtraction of items isn't an easy job but it can be done. It will take you a lot of time, hard work and dedication, but it is possible. It is each generation's responsibility to improve the contents of their bag before it is passed down to the next generation.

Each generation has the opportunity to carefully look at its contents and choose one (or two if you are game) items to eliminate and one (or two) items to add or strengthen. It would be impossible for one person to tackle every negative item themselves. If each generation tackles one the backpack will continue to get stronger.

Yesterday I was talking to a lovely woman at the hairdressing salon. She had recently separated from her husband and like all good parents was concerned about its impact on her two soon to be teenage children. Her husband had struggled with a severe pornography addiction for years and it had taken its toll on every area of their lives. They had exhausted their options of working through the issue together so they decided to separate.

A few of her family members had asked her why she wouldn't stay for the sake of her children. She had thought through that carefully. She didn't want to stay in a relationship that she wouldn't want her children to stay in. She felt that it was a bad example. She didn't want her children to think it was normal to argue constantly about sex, finances and the numerous other areas it affected. She wanted to show them that marriage should be based on trust and respect.

There was so much about this situation that this mother couldn't take responsibility for. So much of it was outside of her control. However, when this brave mum looked in her backpack she decided to own what she could. The number one item she wanted to own and overcome was a sense of failure.

This mother felt that her primary responsibility as a parent was to provide a stable and safe home for her children. When that wasn't there, it forced her to admit to herself and to her kids that she felt like a failure. If she chose not to take responsibility for it she feared she would pass this sense of failure down to her children.

A feeling of failure is a big thing for parents to work through. Parents want their children to think they have it all together. Instead of being able to be seen as perfect this mother had to be prepared to be seen as less than perfect. "Perhaps, given some time, some consistency and love your teenager will see you as real, responsible, brave and strong. This could be argued as being even better than perfect," I argued.

Admitting to feelings of failure was the single most important step in guiding her beautiful children through the very difficult and painful process that lay ahead. Great parents are not perfect parents. They are parents who say, "The buck stops with me. This is my load and no matter how tough it is I am going to carry it." If nothing else great parents pass down an attitude that says, "I can overcome the challenges that life throws at me."

The backpack concept goes horribly wrong when parents fail to take responsibility for the negatives in their backpack. I notice some parents carry around a load, which they feel is too heavy for them to do anything about. They feel outweighed by inherited hardship they didn't ask for. It could be poverty, sickness, broken relationships or a history of abuse. They are literally overburdened and squashed by their backpacks. It paralyses them, sometimes in many areas, other times only in one area.

What they often don't realise is that if they don't deal with the contents of their bag they are actually handing it down to their children to deal with. When we fail to deal with our problems they become our children's problem. That means if that mum had chosen to ignore or wallow in her sense of failure her children would have been far worse off for it. Every generation needs to conquer something for the sake of the generation coming after them.

Many children have to deal with things that their parents truly wish they didn't have to bear. They wish the backpack they had given their children was lighter. The truth is that we can't give our children everything and we can't conquer everything for them. There are children all over our country who are facing the pain of divorce and no one else can deal with that pain for them except them. The very best we can give them is a conquering attitude. We can provide for them an example of someone who has overcome their own lot in life.

Sports psychology tells us that the heavier the backpack that someone is carrying the more it impedes their vision. They are less likely to be able to see as clearly or as far as someone who is carrying a lighter load. Without a clear vision for their future our daughters will really struggle to stay on track in life and climb their big mountains.

What has this got to do with my daughter partying you may ask? What are you getting at Michelle? Our children mirror our behaviour. In many cases our teenagers copy us and the way we handle stress. If we are taking responsibility for looking after ourselves it gives our children a better chance of handling their stress responsibly. Don't tell them not to drink when you are drunk every second weekend. It won't work. Don't lecture them about smokes when you are puffing on one. We don't want them to be using alcohol and drugs as a way of backing off from their problems so we have to be careful how we are coping with ours.

STRATEGY 1:

Look at Yourself First

When parents come to my office they come for a reason. The reason is usually Kate, their adorable daughter who has turned 14 has made their life a waking mess. So I, the genius problem shooter, ask the obvious question, "What is the problem?" There are a lot of parents who give me the quick, to-the-point summarised answer, "She is the problem." Black and white, start and finish. Kate is the beginning and the end of the problem.

Although on the surface this seems to sum things up it does disturb me when parents don't admit to contributing anything to the dramas that are happening at home. It wouldn't be humanly possible to not be doing something to make the situation worse. It does take two to tango and parents are often at their wits end with being so frustrated.

Great parents know that they are not necessarily to blame for their daughters' choices but they also know they aren't perfect. Great parents don't isolate their teenagers' problems like they have nothing to do with them. Great parents know that they always have something to do with them. Always! They are always the first ones to put up their hand and admit it.

Relationships are funny things. They involve everyone. We are inter-twined with each other and as much as we would like to be autonomous family just doesn't operate like that. We affect each other. That is why great parents have what I like to call 'generational thinking'. They don't just think in terms of themselves, they don't just think in terms of their family. They think in terms of their entire generational line. They talk about their family in extended terms, not just immediate terms.

Ask yourself:

- How do I handle my life's challenges?
- How do I talk about my life's challenges?
- How do I use alcohol?
- How do I use drugs?
- How do I use cigarettes and other addictive substances?
- Do I have consistent values when it comes to drugs and alcohol?
- Do I take care of my health?
- How well am I carrying my backpack?

Mums Write In...

I have three children and have always made it a rule never, never, ever to get drunk in front of them. They know we have a glass of wine a few times a year, but never to the stage that they see us out of control. This would be setting such a bad example and one that could potentially blow up in our faces later down the track. I have also never bought my daughter alcohol and told her I never would. My daughter finished Year 12 last year and of course was well and truly ready for her schoolies experience. We stuck to our guns and decided not to buy her alcohol. I asked her once she arrived safely home (and believe me you just want them home in one piece) how she got her alcohol because she told me that she was going to drink. She admitted that it was easy. There were plenty of over 18s hanging around bottle shops willing to take their money, buy them their alcohol and take a bottle or two for their efforts.

STRATEGY 2:

Stay Calm

A mother once rang me totally distraught that she had found a packet of cigarettes in her daughter's room. (You can replace cigarettes for alcohol, marijuana or any other drug you like.) She had never expected her daughter to smoke and thought smoking cigarettes was a disgusting habit. It was around lunchtime and she had approximately three hours before her daughter arrived home. She was counting down, pacing the floor and rehearsing the perfect disapproval speech.

I had to admire her passion for the issue as she had well and truly put some thought into it. She had prepared educational information to give to her daughter—kind of like a mini assignment—which contained information printed from the Internet. She had made sure she had printed the scariest mouth, throat and lung cancer photos possible just for added effect. I got the impression she thought she might even think her daughter had already contracted throat cancer.

She had rung to express her concern and ask for my advice. I bravely asked her to pretend I was her daughter and practice on me. "Let me have it!" I said. So with notes in hand she began. It was like hearing a racing car fly into first gear! She was off and running. For my own amusement I let her go for it. She went on (five minutes later) and on (10 minutes later) and on (15 minutes later) and on (20 minutes later). At this point I tried to interrupt but it was honestly like trying to hold back the tide so I just let her go for it. I had definitely been told off and was sure I would never smoke another cigarette again in my lifetime.

"How was that?" she asked.

"Impressive," I replied honestly. "But I have one concern. All those words are likely to cause a huge argument in your household tonight. I would love to see you confront your daughter and get the same results without a huge argument that might end up in grief for everyone. Would you be open to trying another idea?" I could hear her hesitancy. I could honestly understand why. She had invested so much in that speech and it was impressive, well researched, direct and passionate.

I decided to continue in an attempt to win her over. "Heather, the way we handle things as parents can either soothe a situation or make it worse. Sometimes strong words and emotion aggravate an already tense situation. Your daughter has broken your trust and made an unwise decision but she may be really struggling and need your support. The more that you say out of frustration the more opportunity there is for the wrong thing to be said. Arguments usually happen because too much is said too quickly.

"Can I get you to peel things back a little? Instead of delivering that speech (and the mini-assignment) would you simply put the cigarettes on the bench and say, 'I found these in your room today. I'd like to hear what you have to say about them when you are ready. Your father and I will need to talk to you about consequences once we have heard from you', and then do nothing but wait. Stop Talking! Full stop. Ball is in her court. There is no ranting or raving on your part."

I could hear what Heather was thinking... she deserves to be told off! I really WANT to tell her off. I asked Heather which would be more effective (and better for her other children): disciplining her with lots of words or a few words. Which would aggravate the situation: more emotion or less emotion?

Parents always tend to talk too much and over react when they get worried, frustrated or angry. They somehow think that their daughters need to know what they are thinking and how they are feeling. I don't quite know why that is. It's like parents haven't quite registered that their teenagers don't actually care too much about their perspective. It's far better for parents to take a step back and breathe and do everything they can to keep the situation calm.

Great parents make sure they process their feelings away from their daughter so they are not excessively emotional when they are interacting with their daughter. When parents are afraid or angry they often say things that they will later regret. The more that is said the more opportunity there is for the wrong thing to be said.

It is my pleasure to say that Heather decided to talk less, which enabled her daughter to talk more. She had a great heart felt, connected conversation with her daughter about lying and cigarettes... that led to talking about pressure from friends and drugs. This conversation wouldn't have happened if her mother met her ranting and raving. She still got grounded, and her daughter still chucked a mental about it, but at the end of the day they stayed connected as a family. That is what matters most of all.

Parents, please remember that when the volume goes up in your household you are losing control, regardless of who is doing the yelling. The worst thing you can do is to make the situation more tense simply because you are frustrated. Parents often confuse discipline with creating a tense and stressful environment. Keep calm and stay in control of your own emotions. It is so, so important if you want your teenager to respect you at the end of the day.

Mums Write In...

I have struggled with anxiety since childhood and take anti-anxiety medication every day. For me this strategy is something that I relate to. I am not sure that I rant and rave like this mother but my kids would tell you that I worry about things that I don't need to. I have to make sure that I am not micro-managing their lives out of fear. I just wanted to write to you Michelle because there are so many mothers who suffer from anxiety and I believe it has a big impact on parenting and how we see our children.

STRATEGY 3:

Develop a Safety Plan

Parties are the perfect place for a teenager to let their hair down and many teenagers spend all week planning how they are going to outsmart their parents in order to have the maximum amount of fun possible. What we want to do is give them enough space to rebel safely so they get it out of their system, without all the nasty consequences.

These are the questions you need to ask to ensure their safety before you say 'yes' to a party.

Basics: Where is it? When is it? Whose party is it? Why is the party being held?

Party Host: Is there an adult in charge? Can I speak to them? If not, why not.

Supervision: How many teenagers will be attending? How much adult supervision will be supplied? Will there be alcohol? If so who is supplying it and how much? Do you have a plan if things get out of hand?

The Big Picture: Do you have any concerns? Do you feel comfortable?

Whenever your teenager leaves the house they are representing your family. Even though you can't control what she does when she is away from you, there should be some clear expectations of how you expect her to behave. These rules are very much based on your family values but here are some good thoughts. Don't do it if it's illegal. Don't do it if it's immoral. Don't do it if it's dangerous. Don't do it if you won't be proud of yourself in the morning.

Agree on a drop off and pick up time. Agree to wait out the front of the party for your teenager but tell them you will come in (and possibly embarrass them greatly) if they are late. I once knew a mum who deliberately picked up her daughter in Ugg boots and PJs because she was tired of her daughter making her wait.

I always like the idea of teenagers going to a party with people you know will have their backs. The idea of 'never leave your mates' can't be reinforced enough. Far less can go wrong if young people take care of each other.

If your teenager telephones you because he or she is in trouble agree to pick them up and get them home without having an argument about it then and there. Forget who is right and wrong and just bring them home!

Similarly, I say to my children no matter what situation you find yourself in, do whatever you need to do to come home safely. If there is something we need to sort out afterwards we can fight that battle then. I'll pay the bill. Just get home.

Make sure your daughter has three emergency contact numbers in her phone. These should be people she can call anytime. She should also have the number for a taxi in her emergency contact list.

Every teenager needs to be able to blame their parent in order to get out of an unsafe or tricky situation. That's where family emergencies come in handy. For example, if your daughter needs to get picked up from a party but doesn't want to look silly in front of her friend she can say, "Mum says there's been an emergency and she has to pick me up in 15 minutes. She won't tell me what it is until she gets me." You can work out what the emergency is later. Teenagers love emergencies!

I prefer teenagers to not drink alcohol at all. If you are not of this opinion please agree on an amount of alcohol your teenager should drink and supply it for them rather than have them get it from older friends. If you suspect your daughter has drunk more alcohol than the agreed upon amount (or taken drugs for that matter) you can breath or drug test your teenager and make it a prerequisite for going to parties. You can buy breath or drug tests from many pharmacies.

My opinion is that you would never let your daughter stay the night at the place where the party is being held. Chances are that other parents aren't as attentive as you and the after party is where all the real action happens.

Prior to saying 'yes' to the party is the perfect time to slip in some extra education around alcohol, drugs and sex. Your daughter is likely to listen to anything you have to say during this time. She has no choice but to put up with it then so milk it for all it's worth.

Mums Write In...

My daughter has been to many parties over the years and I can still remember the first sleep over she was invited to in year one. She was six years-old and we didn't know the family. There were both boys and girls invited, (heaps of them which would have been too many for me to handle) which I couldn't believe. What shocked me the most was that every second child was allowed to stay the night. We allowed her to go to the party, get changed into her nightie and hang out until 7.30pm. We told her we would pick her up and take her home. It didn't go down very well... My six year-old stormed out of the party and sulked all the way in the car on the way home. We did explain to her that we didn't know the family and it would be better that we knew them first. After half way home we got really annoyed at her whinging; I decided to pull the car over outside a random house. She looked at me strangely. "What are you doing?" she asked. "I want you to get out, knock on the door and ask them if you can stay the night." She was shocked and said, "But I don't know the people!" "Exactly," I said. "And I don't know your friend's family either, that's why you are coming home." She never said another word and I enjoyed the rest of the car ride home.

STRATEGY 4:

Watch for Warning Signs

Research says that YOU are one of the most powerful influences in your teenager's life when it comes to preventing them from taking drugs[99]. Talking to your teenager about your expectations regarding drug use is critical but may not be necessary until they are at an age that it is relevant in their world. That means that for most young people sometime after 13 years of age is a good time to start to address this issue more seriously. That doesn't mean that some children (who have had exposure to drug use or have an inquisitive mind) don't have the maturity to discuss it earlier.

I always take the health angle when it comes to discussing drugs. Explain that you want them to stay healthy in their body and mind and that the best way to do that is to stay completely away from drugs (and in my opinion, alcohol). Acknowledge that there is a lot of temptation out there and that it is an area that you will need to communicate a lot about.

It is also important to discuss the values and attitudes behind drug use. Drugs are a quick hit but not a long-term answer. Real life rewards good choices but it doesn't always reward them instantly. It is critical that we teach our children that we don't always get rewarded straight away in life. Sometimes we have to do things because they are the right thing to do, not because we are going to get rewarded for it. The rewards that life gives us are not instant, but they are lasting.

Drug use steals purpose while the real world rewards good performance. You get a job, a pay rise and healthy relationships because you input into them. If we reward our young people for doing nothing and contributing nothing, we are setting them up for failure. We have to teach our daughters how the real world works by modelling it in our homes. We can't accommodate a purposeless, drug-centred lifestyle in our homes.

Keep reinforcing the power of their choice. When I ask a teenager, "Why did you do that?" the response I would like to get is, "Because it is the right thing to do." That would be my ultimate. Not because I will look good in front of my friends or because it makes me feel good. Just simply it's the right thing to do and I know that if I do the right thing the real world rewards these choices. Full stop.

Explain that you will always take a strong stand when it comes to drugs. You can't control what your teenager does when they go out but you can control what they do at home. If you find drugs in your home call the police. Don't negotiate. I also tell parents to express their concerns clearly and firmly, especially when it comes to drug use at home. Set firm boundaries. This is the hardest part and a moral dilemma for many parents who are torn between trying to keep a girl safe by keeping her at home and being clear about their position with drugs.

The better informed your teenager is about the science behind drugs the safer they will be. You can't stop your daughters from coming across drugs but you can educate them. Books and other educational tools, including good bloggers and 'Youtubers' are worth keeping an eye out for.

Research says that 4.8% of 12-13 year-olds have tried

marijuana, which rises to 26.7% of 16-17 year olds[100.] I personally think it's more common than parents realise. Cannabis is so readily available to teenagers. They can literally get it anywhere. I hear that the going price is $25 for approximately 700grams or a quarter of an ounce, which makes up about four joints. This is very cheap and totally affordable for any teenager. So, my point is this: parents, we need to keep our eyes open. All kids have the opportunity to smoke pot these days.

Cannabis is more commonly known as 'marijuana', 'pot', 'weed', 'dope', 'mr green' and 'grass'. There is also a range of synthetic cannabinoids, chemical compounds found in cannabis that are equally as popular and are used in a similar way. A key ingredient in marijuana, THC, damages those areas of the brain, which are responsible for memory and learning. I have seen this in action. When I speak at alternative learning schools I often see young people who have lost their mind by using pot, which is so incredibly sad when they are only 15.

Be aware of the signs of smoking pot:

- Skipping school
- Not coming home at the arranged time
- Lying
- Missing cash / unaccounted for money
- Misplaced items
- Unusual items
- Jumpy, angry, irritable, mood swings
- Isolated / staying in room
- Bloodshot eyes
- Evasive

Dealing with a teenager who is experimenting with pot takes

skilful parenting and often professional support. Parents often 'know' before they know (if you know what I mean). Trust your instincts but also try and find evidence so you have concrete proof of drug use. It is also important that parents are realistic about why their daughter is smoking marijuana. Are they anxious or depressed or stressed or just trying to fit in? The most challenging part is to find healthy alternatives and keep them busy and purposeful.

Mums Write In...

My daughter had the opportunity to assist with a program that connects homeless people with community services that they would otherwise not have access to, such as legal advice, medical care, accommodation and clothing. She was in Year 11 at the time. What she brought home from that experience was the witness of what drugs and alcohol could do to a young person and their family. She was shocked at the fact that a young mum was homeless and that drugs and alcohol were almost always linked to their stories. This, I felt, was such a direct source of education for her and really reinforced all the issues that the school and we should discuss about the negative impact of drugs and alcohol. It was a priceless experience for her.

STRATEGY 5:

Remember Back When

You might remember what it was like to be a teenager but might not be able to recall the feelings associated with that time in your life. Once those intense emotions leave your system there is no returning to them. You quickly forget how foggy your thinking was and how important it was to please your friends. Remembering is hard because we only remember what we want to remember. We have a selective memory.

Our daughters' experiences may look so much different than our own, but it is hard to tell how much different they really are. We can't actually jump into our parent's bodies and see ourselves through their eyes. We did stupid things too. Sometimes it is worth remembering that kids will be kids and probably make it through just fine. What are the teenage years without a few good stories of getting busted by your parents anyway?

I often remind parents that it is unlikely that your daughter is going to be giving you the finger at 30. It is far more likely that they will be asking for your advice and maybe even your help to pay the mortgage. Her problems will grow into adult size problems. So next time you are horrified at her behaviour try and remember back when you were young and stupid. It might put things into perspective. Remember that you grew up in the process of time and she is likely to as well.

Mums Write In...

My daughter is in Year 8 and she asked if her friend Annie could stay the night. I said 'yes' because I'm always happy when she is at home because I can keep an eye on her. I remember the car pulling up and I began to walk towards my door to meet Annie's mum and have the talk about what time she needed to be home in the morning and what she was allowed and not allowed to do. I was going to have the 'responsible mum' talk. No sooner had I opened the door then Annie's lift took off down the street! Annie walked in and that was that. I couldn't believe it. Here I had another person's 13 year-old daughter in my home for the next sixteen hours and they didn't know me from a bar of soap. The next morning Annie's mum rang the doorbell and stood there ready to collect her daughter. Too bad by that stage if I was some sort of sexual offender! No wonder my daughter thinks I am absolutely embarrassing when I interview parents before I allow her to stay over. I really don't understand how people can be so relaxed when it comes to sleepovers and putting their children in other people's care. Parents are relying on their children to make decisions about their safety and ring them if they are in trouble. I mean, what if their phone isn't working for some reason? I rarely allow sleepovers and I like to know where my kids are.

STRATEGY 6:

Parent Your Own Child

I sat with a girl today who was holding onto a secret that was troubling her. I would have preferred that she spoke to her mum about it but instead she asked her mum to bring her to my counselling centre to confidentially talk to me. We left mum in the waiting room nervously fidgeting, wondering what the problem could be.

She told me that her friend was planning to smoke drugs at a party on the weekend. She had a strong conviction about drugs and was really worried about it. She was worried about her friend's safety and reputation. I have been around long enough to know that not everything that teenagers talk about eventuate, so we took things slowly.

We talked through the difference between the roles of being a friend and a mother. I made sure she knew she wasn't her mother or even an adult. She was a kid. We also talked about the advice she was currently giving her friend. She was rating herself as A+ and so was I.

Next up we talked through what to do if she was at a party and there were drugs, or if a friend had taken drugs and became unwell or unresponsive. She felt prepared. She was taking responsibility for herself. I was happy.

The saddest bit for me was that she didn't want to speak to her mum, just in case she spoke to her friend's mum about it. She desperately wanted to talk to her mum but didn't want to risk her mum passing on this information. I had an opportunity to talk to her mum about how her daughter needed to confide in her. Years ago a mum told me that she would tell her daughter, "You can tell your friend you will tell nobody. I am Mr Nobody." I think this is good advice.

Parents often ask me if they should notify a teenager's parent if they discover another child has done or is about to do something inappropriate. This is a tough call if you know the other mum really well. Obviously there are no blanket rules and every situation calls for a different response. You have to put your own head on the pillow at night and be able to sleep.

However over the years I have discovered that it is far better to keep your nose out of other children's lives unless it is a life-threatening affair. Time after time I have found that truth that needs to be uncovered comes to light all by itself. Good intentions usually backfire. Good meaning parents who offer their 'help' often find out that their information is not welcomed in the same spirit given. You can also alienate your own child by not being exclusively on their team. I always say to my kids, "I am *your* mum, not everyone else's."

As a general rule exclusively parent your own child rather than other people's. This will enable your child to confide in you. It also allows you to exclusively be on their team.

Mums Write In...

I am a good friend of one of my daughter's friend's mums. The thought of not speaking to her about something that could potentially harm her daughter is almost sickening to me. I found this strategy really confronting and I have been thinking about it a lot, especially in light of where my daughter is at in her life. The other day there was an incident where my daughter didn't speak to me because of this very thing. She had left her friend at the shops (they were supposed to be shopping together) and rung me to come home early. When I asked what had happened she said, "I can't tell you cause you will tell her mum." I didn't like that, so I take your point Michelle. When they are little it is okay to share information with other mums, but there is a time when they grow up and there is more at stake. I'm not prepared to get pushed out of my daughter's life for the sake of my friendship with another mum.

STRATEGY 7:

Negotiation 101

Some kids learn on the job, meaning they learn from their mistakes. It is very difficult to watch a child learn the hard way, but for some girls that is the ONLY way they will learn. All the nagging in the world isn't going to teach them anything. Parents of strong-willed girls have a big job on their hands. They work hard at communicating, coaching and on some occasions, fighting for their teenagers' safety.

This visual, used by many professionals, is a great way to explain to strong willed teenagers how much decision-making power they have and don't have. The more strong-willed a girl is the earlier she will want to make decisions independently. For other children they will prefer the security of having their parents make those decisions for them or in partnership with them.

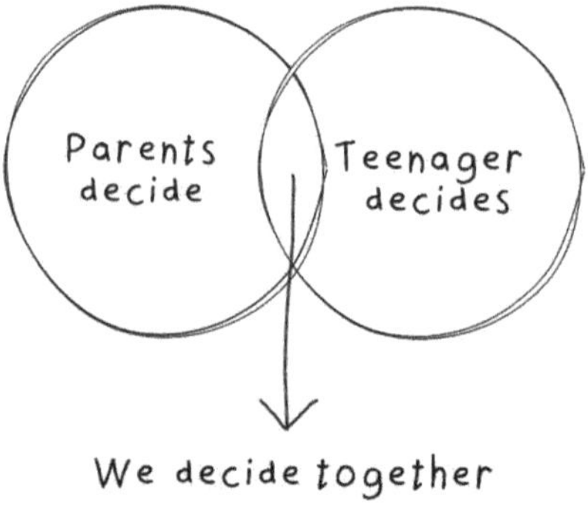

Being given the opportunity to 'decide' doesn't mean they have a ticket to ultimate freedom. That's the catch. They still have to be accountable for their decision. For example, they may get to choose what time they go to bed on the weekend but also be accountable to ensure they are up at a reasonable time to participate in whatever family activities are happening. If your daughter isn't ready to own the outcome she isn't ready to own the decision.

Even when a parent has given their daughter the right to make decisions they are still within their right to talk them through questions like these that will help keep them accountable for their decision-making process:

- What do you think you need to do?
- Do you know all the facts?
- Are you sure of the consequences?
- What decision have you made?
- What is the outcome?
- Did it work?
- Who was affected?
- What is the next decision you need to make?

Mums Write In...

These are the rules we negotiated for my two girls who were different ages and were comparing themselves to each other (especially the younger one who wanted lots of freedom early). She needed to know clearly what she was and wasn't allowed to do.

Sarah's Rules (12 – 14 years-old):

You always need supervision by an adult.

We will always need to ask you questions to assess the

level of supervision. I will need more details from you than your sister. If we don't get clear answers the answer will be no.

The following people count as supervision: parents, youth leader (not just helpers) and Joanne. Who doesn't count – Joanne's friends or any other young adults.

Joanne's Rules (16 years-old):

You don't need adult supervision.

We love to see you socialise with kids who are making sensible choices. You can go out as much as you want.

We won't stop you going out unless you are in an unsafe or unhealthy environment:

- *alcohol*
- *drugs*
- *hooking up*
- *blatant disrespect*
- *dangerous or irresponsible driving*
- *pornography or excessive rude language.*

We are most concerned about your choices, happiness and relationship with us. If we have concerns it will be because we are concerned about one of these areas.

Curfew: 11.30pm - 12.00am on weekends.

In the weekdays we want your priority to be your sport, work or music commitments unless there is something special on.

Communication: Who you are going with and where you are going (in general)?

STRATEGY 8:

Encourage Purpose

Developing a healthy and productive lifestyle undergirds EVERYTHING that I do in my work with teenagers. The happier and healthier young people are within themselves, the more likely they are to make positive life choices. Tennis, swimming, dance, soccer, netball... anything that keeps them active and alive is great. You can also try part time work, music lessons, drama classes, youth groups or evening TAFE courses that keep them busy.

Finding positive things for them to do can be more difficult than it sounds. With both parents often working around the clock and young people often left unattended it is harder and harder for parents to structure positive activity. Xbox or social media is usually the easiest, most convenient way for young people to entertain themselves. It can be a vicious cycle.

Exploring interests while they are young (and keen) does give them more options as they get older. So if you have a primary school aged child and are reading this book now is the time to encourage extracurricular activities. Our daughters are not always known for their motivation, so getting a young person moving in a positive direction if they are at a standstill can be difficult. It is far easier to get them moving in a positive direction as pre-teens and keep them moving that way through their teenage years. Keeping positive momentum and small wins in teenagers' lives is so, so important.

Our daughters may try all sorts of ways to get attention, including experimenting with their appearance, their clothes or finding new interests. What I love to see is a young person who finds a 'positive grab' that they are known for, whether that be playing drums, sports or academic achievement. You can't underestimate the importance of a teenager finding their own reason to get up in the morning. They need a reason to feel confident about who they are. When teenagers find purpose for themselves and are motivated from within, rather than by outside sources, it is bliss for parents.

So on a practical level I encourage you to find one or two positive activities for your young person to be involved in and make the financial and time sacrifices it takes to keep them engaged in those areas. Keep them as busy as possible with positive things. If you need to bribe them in order to get them engaged in something, do it. Pull out all stops to keep their lives moving in a positive direction. This is by far the best strategy for helping young people make healthy choices that I know. A healthy mind is supported by a healthy lifestyle. A healthy lifestyle is more likely to be undertaken with healthy company and influences.

Mums Write In...

My goal as a parent is to keep my teenagers as busy as possible and as worn out as possible that they don't have any time to get themselves into trouble. Yes, that means that I will be worn out too (and broke!) and that I won't have any free time to have fun, but I'd rather that than be concerned about their safety. If I can keep them busy doing things that they love and things that they are good at surely it will minimise the time they have to get into trouble in the first place.

Concluding Thoughts

I would like to leave you with these thoughts. Parenting is all about doing your best with the knowledge and understanding you have at the time. My hope is that this book has provided a little more knowledge and understanding.

As you use the strategies in this book there may be times when you feel overwhelmed with the task of parenting a teenager. Maybe your teenager will get involved in sexting or drugs. Maybe they will be kicking the front door down wanting to stay out all night or maybe, just maybe, your daughter won't give you any trouble at all and you will be reading this book wondering what all the fuss is about.

Some strategies will really hit the mark and the reality is some may not produce the results you expected. It's during these frustrating and disappointing times that you most need encouragement to keep making decisions and pushing things forward. A sense of confidence and reassurance is the number one thing that parents need in order to keep their parenting on track. You need to know that ALL parents are in the same boat! But where do parents get their confidence topped up when they are under pressure?

Parents often look to each other for support and answers. A parent's need for reassurance is the reason you can go into any coffee shop any day of the week and find groups of mothers talking about their parenting. They are hoping to hear those uplifting words, "Gosh I wish I had as much patience as you do! You are a saint!;" or "You are so organised. How do you manage to do all that you do? You are such a great mum!" And although we would all ideally love our teenagers to sit us down and say, "You know the way you disciplined me last week... it showed real courage and conviction. It was amazing." We all know that isn't likely to happen!

So let me replace the teenager, the partner, the mum, the friend, or whoever you wish would give you some encouragement and feedback on your parenting by telling you right now that if you are still making decisions, if you are still emotionally engaged, if you still care, you are doing a great job. If you are using the tools in front of you with all of your heart you are awesome.

So mums, next time you are slaving over the kitchen sink (washing the dishes from the meal you have just lovingly prepared) and you hear your daughter slam her bedroom door in disgust because you won't let her stay up texting all night... remind yourself that you are irreplaceable in your child's life and that she doesn't fully realise your worth (or the value of sleep and time).

And dads next time you have driven your daughter to late night shopping (when you were tired and would rather be watching TV) and she has called you the worst parent in the world because you didn't buy her the new dress she wanted... remember your daughter may not have everything she wants but she has you, a dedicated father that many girls crave. In time she will come to appreciate it.

And finally I want to say this. When parents come to me and they feel like they have 'done everything' and are 'stuck' I say to them, "Just *slowly* take ground." If you feel like your teenager won't communicate with you and shuts you out of her life your job is to slowly creep into her heart. You want to know that this time next year you have made progress. You want to know that when she turns eighteen you are in a better position. If you gain ground slowly she won't realise that you are doing it and it won't create as many waves.

Many parents try to turn things around before Friday, which simply doesn't work. Allow it to happen steadily inch by inch... let your love creep up on her.

That's all from me.

Michelle

About Michelle Mitchell

Michelle worked as a teacher before establishing Youth Excel, a charity that helps young people make positive life choices during difficult times. As a national speaker Michelle has a unique ability to transfer years of knowledge and experience to people of all ages and professions. In 2013 Michelle was awarded Inspirational Women Speaker of the Year by the Queensland State Government. Michelle is recognised as a teenage expert. Her innovative work has been featured on The Today Show, Today Tonight, Channel Ten Morning News, 96.5fm, ABC radio, The Melbourne Age, Women's Weekly, The Courier Mail and countless other print media. Michelle is married and has two teenagers. She lives in Brisbane, Australia.

Visit **www.michellemitchell.org**

About Youth Excel

Youth Excel is an innovative charity, which exists to enhance the mental health and wellbeing of young people. We are committed to early intervention and prevention with the goal of seeing young people transition well into adulthood and reach their full potential. It is a privilege to say that we reach thousands of young people each year through our psychology, counselling and mentoring services.

For more information about our clinic, school programs and resources visit our website **www.youthexcel.com.au**

Endnotes

I HAVE MET YOUR DAUGHTER

1 Green, L., Brady, D., Olafsson, K., Hartley, J., & Lumby, C. (2011). *Risks and safety for Australian children on the Internet: Full findings from the AU Kids Online survey of 9–16 year olds and their parents.* Kelvin Grove: ARC Centre of Excellence for Creative Industries and Innovation and EU Kids Online. Retrieved from ←https://www.ecu.edu.au/__data/assets/pdf_file/0009/294813/U-Kids-Online-Survey.pdf→

2 Lee, M., Crofts, T., McGovern, A., & Milivojevic. (2015). *Sexting among young people: Perceptions and Practices. Trends and Issues in Crime and Criminal Justice, 508.* Australian Institute of Criminology, Canberra.

3 Lawrence, D., Johnson, S., Hafekost, J., Botorhoven de Haan, K., Sawyer, M., Ainley, J. & Zubrick, S. R. (2015) *Report on the second Australian Child and Adolescent Survey of Mental Health and Wellbeing.* Department of Health, Canberra.

4 Mitchell, A., Patrick, K., Heywood, W., Blackman, P., & Pitts, M. (2014). National survey of Australian secondary students and sexual health 2013. *Melbourne: Australian Research Centre in Sex Health and Society & La Trobe University.*

5 Hemphill, S. A., Tollit, M., & Kotevski, A. (2012). Rates of bullying perpetration and victimisation: A longitudinal study of secondary school students in Victoria, Australia. *Pastoral Care in Education, 30*(2), 99-112.

6 Lawrence, D., Johnson, S., Hafekost, J., Botorhoven de Haan, K., Sawyer, M., Ainley, J. & Zubrick, S. R. (2015) *Report on the second Australian Child and Adolescent Survey of Mental Health and Wellbeing.* Department of Health, Canberra.

7 DiVall, S. A., & Radovick, S. (2009). Endocrinology of female puberty. *Current Opinion in Endocrinology, Diabetes and Obesity, 16*(1), 1-4.

DISRESPECT

8 Tully, J. (2014). On Global Citizenship: James Tully in Dialogue. Bloomsbury Academic, 92.

9 UNICEF (2016). UNICEF Data: Monitoring the situation of children and women. Retrieved from: https://data.unicef.org/topic/child-protection/child-labour/#

10 Miller, P., & Bowd, J. (2010). Do Australian teenagers contribute to household work?. *Family Matters*, (85), 68.

11 Roberts – Grey, G. (Year unknown). Help your teen clean up his language. Retrieved from: https://powertochange.com/family/swearing/

12 Cumsille, P., Darling, N., & Martínez, M. L. (2010). Shading the truth: The patterning of adolescents' decisions to avoid issues, disclose, or lie to parents. *Journal of adolescence, 33*(2), 285-296.

13 Darling, N., Cumsille, P., & Martínez, M. L. (2008). Individual differences in adolescents' beliefs about the legitimacy of parental authority and their own obligation to obey: A longitudinal investigation. *Child development, 79* (4), 1103-1118.

14 Australian Institute of Criminology. (2016). Australian crime: facts and figures 2014. Australian Institute of Criminology: Canberra.

15 Australian Institute of Criminology. (2016). Australian crime: facts and figures 2014. Australian Institute of Criminology: Canberra.

16 Australian Institute of Criminology. (2016). Australian crime: facts and figures 2014. Australian Institute of Criminology: Canberra.

17 Dahl, R. (2004). Adolescent brain development: a period of vulnerabilities and opportunities. *Annals of the New York Academy of Sciences*, 1021, 1, 1-22.

SOCIAL MEDIA

18 Houghton, S., Hunter, S. C., Rosenberg, M., Wood, L., Zadow, C., Martin, K., & Shilton, T. (2015). Virtually impossible: limiting Australian children and adolescents daily screen based media use. *BMC public health, 15*(1), 5.

19 Australian Bureau of Statistics. (2013). Australian Health Survey: Physical Activity – 2011 – 2012. Retrieved from: http://www.abs.gov.au/ausstats/abs@.nsf/Latestproducts/4364.0.55.004Main%20Features99992011-12?opendocument&tabname=Summary&prodno=4364.0.55.004&issue=2011-12&num=&view=

20 Office of the Children's eSafety Commissioner. (2016). Research insights: Young and social online. Retrieved from: https://www.esafety.gov.au/about-the-office/research-library

21 The Nielsen Company. (2010). U.S. Teen Mobile Report. Retrieved from: http://www.nielsen.com/us/en/insights/news/2010/u-s-teen-mobile-report-calling-yesterday-texting-today-using-apps-tomorrow.html

22 Office of the Children's eSafety Commissioner. (2016). Research insights: Young and social online. Retrieved from: https://www.esafety.gov.au/about-the-office/research-library

23 Office of the Children's eSafety Commissioner. (2016). Research insights: Young and social online. Retrieved from: https://www.esafety.gov.au/about-the-office/research-library

24 Office of the Children's eSafety Commissioner. (2016). Research insights: Young and social online. Retrieved from: https://www.esafety.gov.au/about-the-office/research-library

25 Office of the Children's eSafety Commissioner. (2016). Research insights: Teens, kids and digital dangers. Retrieved from: https://www.esafety.gov.au/about-the-office/research-library

26 Flood, M. (2007). Exposure to pornography among youth in Australia. *Journal of Sociology*, 43, (1), 45-60.

27 Lee, M., Crofts, T., McGovern, A., & Milivojevic, A. (2015). Sexting and Young People. Criminology Research Grants. Criminology Research Council. Retrieved from: http://www.criminologyresearchcouncil.gov.au/reports/1516/53-1112-FinalReport.pdf

28 Office of the Children's eSafety Commissioner. (2016). Research insights: Teens, kids and digital dangers. Retrieved from: https://www.esafety.gov.au/about-the-office/research-library

29 Coureau, G., Bouvier, G., Lebailly, P., Fabbro-Peray, P., Gruber, A., Leffondre, K., ... & Baldi, I. (2014). Mobile phone use and brain tumours in the CERENAT case-control study. *Occupational and environmental medicine, 71*(7), 514-522.

30 Lee, M., Crofts, T., McGovern, A., & Milivojevic, A. (2015). Sexting and Young People. Criminology Research Grants. Criminology Research Council. Retrieved from: http://www.criminologyresearchcouncil.gov.au/reports/1516/53-1112-FinalReport.pdf

SEXUALITY

31 Mitchell, A., Patrick, K., Heywood, W., Blackman, P., & Pitts, M. (2014). National survey of Australian secondary students and sexual health 2013. *Melbourne: Australian Research Centre in Sex Health and Society & La Trobe University.*

32 Mitchell, A., Patrick, K., Heywood, W., Blackman, P., & Pitts, M. (2014). National survey of Australian secondary students and sexual health 2013. *Melbourne: Australian Research Centre in Sex Health and Society & La Trobe University.*

33 Mitchell, A., Patrick, K., Heywood, W., Blackman, P., & Pitts, M. (2014). National survey of Australian secondary students and sexual health 2013. *Melbourne: Australian Research Centre in Sex Health and Society & La Trobe University.*

34 Mitchell, A., Patrick, K., Heywood, W., Blackman, P., & Pitts, M. (2014). National survey of Australian secondary students and sexual health 2013. *Melbourne: Australian Research Centre in Sex Health and Society & La Trobe University.*

35 Mitchell, A., Patrick, K., Heywood, W., Blackman, P., & Pitts, M. (2014). National survey of Australian secondary students and sexual health 2013. *Melbourne: Australian Research Centre in Sex Health and Society & La Trobe University.*

36 Mitchell, A., Patrick, K., Heywood, W., Blackman, P., & Pitts, M. (2014). National survey of Australian secondary students and sexual health

2013. *Melbourne: Australian Research Centre in Sex Health and Society & La Trobe University.*

37 Cates JR, Herndon NL, Schulz S L, Darroch JE. (2004). Our voices, our lives, our futures: Youth and sexually transmitted diseases. Chapel Hill, NC: University of North Carolina at Chapel Hill School of Journalism and Mass Communication. Retrieved from: http://joancates.web.unc.edu/files/2010/11/Our-Voices-Our-Lives-Our-Futures-Youth-and-Sexually-Transmitted-Diseases.pdf

38 Mitchell, A., Patrick, K., Heywood, W., Blackman, P., & Pitts, M. (2014). National survey of Australian secondary students and sexual health 2013. *Melbourne: Australian Research Centre in Sex Health and Society & La Trobe University.*

39 Flood, M. (2007). Exposure to pornography amongst youth in Australia. *Journal of Sociology*, 43, 1, 45-60.

40 Flood, M. (2009). The Harms of Pornography Exposure Among Children and Young People. *Child Abuse Review, 18, 384 – 400.*

41 Flood, M. (2009). The Harms of Pornography Exposure Among Children and Young People. *Child Abuse Review, 18, 384 – 400.*

42 Grossman, J. M., Frye, A., Charmaraman, L., & Erkut, S. (2013). Family homework and school based sex education: delaying early adolescents' sexual behaviour. *Journal for School Health*, 83, 11, 810 – 817.

43 Mitchell, A., Patrick, K., Heywood, W., Blackman, P., & Pitts, M. (2014). National survey of Australian secondary students and sexual health 2013. *Melbourne: Australian Research Centre in Sex Health and Society & La Trobe University.*

44 Mitchell, A., Patrick, K., Heywood, W., Blackman, P., & Pitts, M. (2014). National survey of Australian secondary students and sexual health 2013. *Melbourne: Australian Research Centre in Sex Health and Society & La Trobe University.*

45 Wight, D., Parkes, A., Strange, V., Allen, E., Bonell, C., & Henderson, M. (2008). The quality of young people's heterosexual relationships: A longitudinal analysis of characteristics shaping subjective experience. *Perspectives on Sexual and Reproductive Health, 40*(4), 226-237.

46 Martino, S. C., Collins, R. L., Elliott, M. N., Kanouse, D. E., & Berry, S. H. (2009). It's better on TV: does television set teenagers up for regret following sexual initiation?. *Perspectives on sexual and reproductive health, 41*(2), 92-100.

47 Tarzon, C. & Quadara, A. (2012). The Nature and Extent of Sexual Assault in Australia. (Resource Sheet). Melbourne [Vic]: Australian Centre for the Study of Sexual Assault

48 Tarzon, C. & Quadara, A. (2012). The Nature and Extent of Sexual Assault in Australia. (Resource Sheet). Melbourne [Vic]: Australian Centre for the Study of Sexual Assault

49 Finkelhor, D., Ormrod, R., & Chaffin, M. (2009). Juveniles Who Commit Sex Offenses Against Minors. *Juvenile Justice Bulletin.*

50 O'Brien, W. (2010). *Australia's response to sexualised or sexually abusive behaviours in children and young people.* Australian Crime Commission.

MOODS

51 Anderson, S. E., & Must, A. (2005). Interpreting the continued decline in the average age at menarche: results from two nationally representative surveys of US girls studied 10 years apart. *The Journal of pediatrics, 147*(6), 753-760.

52 DiVall, S. A., & Radovick, S. (2009). Endocrinology of female puberty. *Current Opinion in Endocrinology, Diabetes and Obesity, 16*(1), 1-4.

53 Lawrence, D., Johnson, S., Hafekost, J., Botorhoven de Haan, K., Sawyer, M., Ainley, J. & Zubrick, S. R. (2015) *Report on the second Australian Child and Adolescent Survey of Mental Health and Wellbeing.* Department of Health, Canberra.

54 Lawrence, D., Johnson, S., Hafekost, J., Botorhoven de Haan, K., Sawyer, M., Ainley, J. & Zubrick, S. R. (2015) *Report on the second Australian Child and Adolescent Survey of Mental Health and Wellbeing.* Department of Health, Canberra.

55 ABS National Survey of Mental Health and Wellbeing: Summary of Results 2007 (2008), p 29

56 Lawrence, D., Johnson, S., Hafekost, J., Botorhoven de Haan, K., Sawyer,

M., Ainley, J. & Zubrick, S. R. (2015) *Report on the second Australian Child and Adolescent Survey of Mental Health and Wellbeing.* Department of Health, Canberra.

57 Mindframe Media (2016). Facts and Stats about Mental Illness in Australia. Retreieved from: http://www.mindframe-media.info/for-mental-health-and-suicide-prevention/talking-to-media-about-mental-illness/facts-and-stats#C&Y

58 Lawrence, D., Johnson, S., Hafekost, J., Botorhoven de Haan, K., Sawyer, M., Ainley, J. & Zubrick, S. R. (2015) *Report on the second Australian Child and Adolescent Survey of Mental Health and Wellbeing.* Department of Health, Canberra.

59 Mindframe Media (2016). Facts and Stats about Mental Illness in Australia. Retreieved from: http://www.mindframe-media.info/for-mental-health-and-suicide-prevention/talking-to-media-about-mental-illness/facts-and-stats#C&Y

60 Kessler RC, Berglund P, Demler O, Jin R, Merikangas KR & Walters EE (2005). Lifetime prevalence and age of onset distributions of DSM-IV Disorders in the National Comorbidity Survey replication. Archives of General Psychiatry, 62, p 593

61 Mullis, I. V. S., Martin, M. O., & Foy, P. (2008). *TIMSS 2007 international mathematics report: Findings from IEA's Trends in International Mathematics and Science Study at the fourth and eighth grades.* Chestnut Hill, MA: TIMSS & PIRLS International Study Center, Boston College.

62 Cross, D., Shaw, T., Hearn, L., Epstein, M., Monks, H., Lester, L., et al. (2009). *Australian Covert Bullying Prevalence Study.* Perth: Child Health Promotion Research Centre, Edith Cowan University. Retrieved from ←education.gov.au/bullying-research-projects#australian-covert-bullying-prevalence→.

63 Joint Select Committee on Cyber-Safety. (2011). *High-wire act: Cyber-safety and the young: Interim report.* Canberra: Parliament of the Commonwealth of Australia. Retrieved from ←www.aph.gov.au/parliamentary_business/committees/house_of_representatives_committees?url=jscc/report.htm→.

64 Spear, L. P. (2000). The adolescent brain and age-related behavioural manifestations. *Neuroscience & Biobehavioral Reviews, 24*(4), 417-463.

65 Holzer, L., Halfon, O., & Thoua, V. (2011). Cerebral maturation in adolescence – teenage brain maturation. *Pediatric Archives*, 18 (5), 579 – 588.

66 Holzer, L., Halfon, O., & Thoua, V. (2011). Cerebral maturation in adolescence – teenage brain maturation. *Pediatric Archives*, 18 (5), 579 – 588.

67 McAnarney, E. R. (2008). Adolescent brain development: Forging new links? *Journal of Adolescent Health*, 42, (4), 321 – 323.

68 Holzer, L., Halfon, O., & Thoua, V. (2011). Cerebral maturation in adolescence – teenage brain maturation. *Pediatric Archives*, 18 (5), 579 – 588.

69 McAnarney, E. R. (2008). Adolescent brain development: Forging new links? *Journal of Adolescent Health*, 42, (4), 321 – 323.

70 Blakemore, S. J., Burnett, S., & Dahl, R. E. (2010). The role of puberty in the developing adolescent brain. *Human brain mapping, 31*(6), 926-933.

71 Giedd, J. N. (2008). The teen brain: insights from neuroimaging. *Journal of Adolescent Health, 42*(4), 335-343.

72 McAnarney, E. R. (2008). Adolescent brain development: Forging new links? *Journal of Adolescent Health*, 42, (4), 321 – 323.

73 DiVall, S. A., & Radovick, S. (2009). Endocrinology of female puberty. *Current Opinion in Endocrinology, Diabetes and Obesity, 16*(1), 1-4.

74 McAnarney, E. R. (2008). Adolescent brain development: forging new links? *The Journal of Adolescent Health*, 42 (4), 321-323.

75 Giedd, J. N. (2008). The teen brain: insights from neuroimaging. *Journal of Adolescent Health, 42*(4), 335-343.

76 Lebel, C., & Beaulieu, C. (2011). Longitudinal development of human brain wiring continues from childhood into adulthood. *Journal of Neuroscience, 31*(30), 10937-10947.

77 Beyond Blue. (2016). What is mental health? Retrieved from: https://www.beyondblue.org.au/the-facts/what-is-mental-health

78 Beyond Blue. (2016). What is mental health? Retrieved from: https://www.beyondblue.org.au/the-facts/what-is-mental-health

79 Lawrence, D., Johnson, S., Hafekost, J., Botorhoven de Haan, K., Sawyer, M., Ainley, J. & Zubrick, S. R. (2015) *Report on the second Australian Child and Adolescent Survey of Mental Health and Wellbeing.* Department of Health, Canberra.

80 Lawrence, D., Johnson, S., Hafekost, J., Botorhoven de Haan, K., Sawyer, M., Ainley, J. & Zubrick, S. R. (2015) *Report on the second Australian Child and Adolescent Survey of Mental Health and Wellbeing.* Department of Health, Canberra.

81 Levesque, R. J. (2010). Special issue introduction: The place of self harm in adolescent development. *The Journal of Youth and Adolescence*, 39 (3), 217-218.

82 Levesque, R. J. (2010). Special issue introduction: The place of self harm in adolescent development. *The Journal of Youth and Adolescence*, 39 (3), 217-218.

83 White, V., & Williams, T. (2016). Australian secondary school students' use of tobacco, alcohol and over the counter and illicit substances in 2014. Centre for Behavioural Research in Cancer Council, Victoria.

84 Herring, R., Bayley, M., & Hurcombe, R. (2014). "But no one told me it's okay to not drink": a qualitative study of young people who drink little or no alcohol. *Journal of Substance Use, 19*(1-2), 95-102.

DRUGS AND ALCOHOL

85 Bailey, V., Baker, A-M., Cave, L., Fildes, J., Perrens, B., Plummer, J. and Wearring, A. 2016, Mission Australia's 2016 Youth Survey Report, Mission Australia.

86 White, V., & Bariola, E. (2011). Australian secondary school students use of tobacco, alcohol and over the counter and illicit substances in 2011. Drug Strategy Branch: Australian Government Department of Health and Ageing.

87 Australian Institute of Health and Welfare. (2013). 2013 National Drug Strategy Household Survey. AIHW, Canberra.

88 Livingston, M. (2015). Understanding recent trends in Australian alcohol

consumption. *Canberra, Australia: Foundation for Alcohol Research and Education.*

89 Hingson, R. W., Heeren, T., & Winter, M. R. (2006). Age at drinking onset and alcohol dependence: age at onset, duration, and severity. *Archives of pediatrics & adolescent medicine, 160*(7), 739-746.

90 Buchmann, A. F., Schmid, B., Blomeyer, D., Zimmermann, U. S., Jennen-Steinmetz, C., Schmidt, M. H., ... & Laucht, M. (2010). Drinking against unpleasant emotions: possible outcome of early onset of alcohol use?. *Alcoholism: Clinical and Experimental Research, 34*(6), 1052-1057.

91 Gross, K. (2008). Gender differences in adolescent risk taking: Are they diminishing?. *Youth Studies Australia, 27*(4), 61-63.

92 Martino, S. C., Collins, R. L., Ellickson, P. L., & Klein, D. J. (2006). Exploring the link between substance use and abortion: The roles of unconventionality and unplanned pregnancy. *Perspectives on Sexual and Reproductive Health, 38*(2), 66-75.

93 Miller, J, Bridle, R & Christou, A (2012). Illicit Drug Use in Western Australia: Australian School Students Alcohol and Drug Survey 2011. Brief communication no.9. Drug and Alcohol Office, Perth.

94 Bridle, R., Christou, A., Miller, J. (2012). Cannabis Trends in Western Australia: ASSAD Survey 2011. Brief communication no.5. Perth: Drug and Alcohol Office.

95 Australian Government National Drug Strategy. (2011). Australian secondary school students' use of tobacco, alcohol, and over-the-counter and illicit substances in 2011. Retrieved from: http://www.nationaldrugstrategy.gov.au/internet/drugstrategy/publishing.nsf/Content/assad-2011~comparisons

96 Australian Institute of Health and Welfare. (2013). 2013 National Drug Strategy Household Survey. AIHW, Canberra.

97 Degenhardt, L., Larney, S., Chan, G., Dobbins, T., Weier, M., Roxburgh, A., ... & McKetin, R. (2016). Estimating the number of regular and dependent methamphetamine users in Australia, 2002–2014. *Medical journal of Australia, 204*(4), 1.

98 Australian Government National Drug Strategy. (2011). Australian secondary school students' use of tobacco, alcohol, and over-the-counter and illicit substances in 2011. Retrieved from: http://www.nationaldrugstrategy.gov.au/internet/drugstrategy/publishing.nsf/Content/assad-2011~comparisons

99 Tobler, A. L., & Komro, K. A. (2010). Trajectories or parental monitoring and communication and effects on drug use among urban young adolescents. *Journal of Adolescent Health, 46*(6), 560-568.

100 Australian Government National Drug Strategy. (2011). Australian secondary school students' use of tobacco, alcohol, and over-the-counter and illicit substances in 2011. Retrieved from: http://www.nationaldrugstrategy.gov.au/internet/drugstrategy/publishing.nsf/Content/assad-2011~comparisons